50 Top Tools for Employee Engagement

50 Top Tools for Employee Engagement

A complete toolkit for improving motivation and productivity

Debbie Mitchell

KoganPage

First published in Great Britain and the United States in 2017 by Kogan Page Limited

2nd Floor, 45 Gee Street	c/o Martin P Hill Consulting	4737/23 Ansari Road
London	122 W 27th Street	Daryaganj
EC1V 3RS	New York, NY 10001	New Delhi 110002
United Kingdom	USA	India

© Debbie Mitchell 2017

The right of Debbie Mitchell to be identified as the author of this work has been asserted by her in accordance with the Copyright, Designs and Patents Act 1988.

ISBN   978 0 7494 7987 9
E-ISBN   978 0 7494 7988 6

British Library Cataloguing-in-Publication Data

A CIP record for this book is available from the British Library.

Library of Congress Control Number
2017001498

Typeset by Integra Software Services, Pondicherry
Print production managed by Jellyfish
Printed and bound in Great Britain by CPI Group (UK) Ltd, Croydon CR0 4YY

For my mum and dad

Together they are a shining example
of true commitment to something that matters.
They demonstrate that it's not always easy,
but prove it's definitely worth the effort.

CONTENTS

ABOUT THE AUTHOR

Debbie Mitchell is an organizational development consultant specializing in employee engagement, coaching, talent management, change and human resource (HR) support. She works with businesses both locally and internationally that include consumer electronics, fast-moving consumer goods (FMCGs) and pharmaceuticals as well as those in the transportation, insurance, not-for-profit and education sectors. Prior to this, Debbie held in-house HR and organizational development (OD) roles for British American Tobacco for 10 years, and has experience of HR roles in retail, public sector and manufacturing.

PREFACE

I've worked as an HR professional for many years. I've worked in a variety of industries and sectors as an in-house personnel manager, HR manager, HR business partner (HRBP) and latterly as a specialist in OD, change management and engagement. Since 2011 I have been working as an independent consultant, facilitator, coach and occasional interim HRBP or OD specialist. My experience has taken me across the public sector, retail, the space business, small manufacturing and FMCG.

My first step in my HR career came thanks to an inspirational boss who recruited me into a small personnel team in the National Health Service (NHS) – my first role out of university – with no substantial experience but a lot of enthusiasm. Early on she inspired me with her own interest in the broader business, not just for traditional personnel activities. She was well respected in the organization; she worked to deliver great service but at the same time contributed to service reviews and trust-wide health-service initiatives as a credible senior leader, not as a token personnel representative contributing solely about the people agenda. She led me to water and encouraged me to drink – within weeks of starting I was getting on with the job. She encouraged and supported me but I was empowered to figure out some of it for myself. She could have left me with interviews and admin – but instead I was covering the full range of (then) personnel services – and then some! Alongside this I was encouraged to work with functional groups and teams on continuous improvement projects – my first attempts with a flipchart and a pen. At the time, we didn't call it facilitation – but it was. And that really was the start of this book.

Over the years, I have facilitated more workshops than I can remember. I have worked with groups for the purposes of team building, problem solving, strategy setting, strategic alignment, business improvement, strategy cascade, innovation, leadership development, project kick-off, project progress reviews, lessons-learnt reviews, group coaching and group mediation. In doing so I have experienced, borrowed, gathered, tweaked and created a range of tools, exercises and activities for various purposes. The portfolio of tools I have been using has grown and evolved over time, and I have found through experience that some can be adapted to use quickly, cost effectively and with good results for employee engagement.

Now operating as a consultant, I work with leadership teams, managers and emerging high-potential talent, and one of the most frequent topics of conversation is about how to engage employees. I have facilitated workshops where I have been told that managers just don't have the time, skill, senior support or resources to do it. This books of tools is intended to bust the myths, to remove all the excuses and to enable managers – and HR professionals – to get on and do something. Simply. Cheaply. Quickly. But effectively.

ACKNOWLEDGEMENTS

A heartfelt thank you to Denise Farmer, for an inspirational start to my career.

Thanks go to all those I have had the privilege of working with over the years since then, during my employed career and as a consultant, using these tools, and others, to facilitate fabulous people.

I have worked with some amazing leaders who have inspired me, as well as some demanding leaders who have challenged me, and in difficult situations that have tested me, and in exciting and positive situations that have motivated me. All have helped me to build a skill set, a wide portfolio, a deep set of experiences, and have inspired me to bring together the tools for this book – I appreciate the trust and empowerment I have been given to work with their challenges, and I appreciate having had the opportunity to learn from them, the good, the bad and the ugly!

My thanks go to all those employees who have willingly – and those who have reluctantly – taken part in workshops, training sessions, kick-offs, away-days and team building. Some have made themselves look daft in the name of development, some have been vulnerable, others have been supportive of team members, and some have been strong advocates of their experiences, of their teams and of their organizations. To all those who have been in a meeting room or open-plan space, and given it a good go, I thank you.

To the amazing Vivienne Palmer, whose initial idea for the Pinspiration board was lovingly stolen and adapted for this book.

I appreciate the help offered by Alan Kelly in trying to identify an IP source for dialogue sheets. Alan's website contains some great information and downloadable examples of dialogue sheets: http://www.allankelly.net/presentations/dialoguesheets.html

Finally, to my husband, for never laughing at my dreams, for reading the book as it developed and for still buying it, even though he knows it inside out!

It is not the intention to claim ownership of any of the individual ideas in this book. They are a collection of tools experienced, created, developed and adapted over my career, and I thank all those who have inspired, contributed and participated. I will be pleased to acknowledge the copyright or origination of any material if this is known.

ABOUT THIS BOOK

Who should use this book?

'In the United Kingdom 17 per cent of employees are engaged, 57 per cent are not engaged and 26 per cent are actively disengaged.' (Gallup 2011–12)

If this statistic surprises or worries you, or if you are not surprised, but recognize the issues it presents, then you need this book.

It is intended for line managers and HR professionals alike. It is written to provide guidance and support at a detailed level to those who might need it, but to additionally provide hints and tips and methods of evaluation to those who have more experience of using such tools.

Whilst primarily targeted at those in small to medium-sized businesses, there may be ideas and suggestions here that will work equally well in large multinationals. There are only a few tools included here that might be better suited to larger organizations – the majority can be adapted for larger or smaller groups as needed, whether that means putting your whole organization into one room for an activity, or breaking your organization into manageable subgroups. The tools offer guidance on when this might be appropriate.

The principle, however, is that as the reader of this tool kit, and as a manager or supervisor in any function, you could implement some tools to help improve employee engagement among your team. Or function. Or the entire workforce.

The philosophy behind the book

Throughout my career, both in-house and as an external consultant, I have facilitated workshops where I have been told that managers just don't have time to promote employee engagement. This book of tools is intended to bust the myths, to remove all the excuses, and to enable managers – and HR professionals – to get on with it. Simply. Cheaply. Quickly. But effectively.

Managers raise concerns with me that they don't know *how* to work on employee engagement. As with many leadership initiatives, it appears to be more complex than it really needs to be. Understanding what it is in very simple terms will help managers to understand the small things that they can do to positively impact employee engagement – but also to keep an eye out for the things they do that might negatively impact it.

Managers would raise concerns about the level of skill or specialist knowledge required to facilitate sessions, and may postpone activity or defer the implementation of engagement initiatives to their HR department if they have one.

I have often heard managers raise concerns that they 'don't have the time' to get involved in employee engagement activities. My response is that you don't need to allocate away-days, or long extended meetings – there are things that you can do in short, sharp but effective time buckets that will build employee engagement. Ideas for engagement activities can span from seconds (a meaningful 'hello' in the morning) to a full away-day – and everything in between.

And finally, when managers have built their knowledge of what employee engagement is, and how they can work on it, they will remind me that they will never get a budget for any such initiatives. Budgets are constrained to some degree in most businesses, and unless there is a clear return on investment, the extra that managers think they need in order to implement employee engagement initiatives will not be forthcoming. And so I remind them that there are so many things that can be done without significant direct cost. Of course all such activities will take time, and that must not be ignored as a cost to the business, but the cost or budget implications should never be a barrier for good employee engagement.

And so, the concept of the book was born – a guide or tool kit that would enable managers, regardless of seniority or specialist knowledge, to identify tools that can help them to increase the levels of engagement among their teams or their workforce, without recourse to specialist consultants, specialist functions, significant budgets or endless days away. Ideally, it wouldn't matter what size or type of organization you work in – the tools are industry agnostic, and whether you lead and manage a small business of five or six people, or work within a multinational industry-leading business, you should find tools and tips in this book that are useful to you.

A particular feature of the book is that it provides some rationale for when and why to use each tool, in that it separates into different sections that highlight when to engage. You will note that engagement, in this context, starts prior to employment, and continues up to and maybe even beyond the point of leaving a business – it covers the full employee life cycle and the changes that happen throughout. It also focuses on some of the key moments, or contacts, for business, and identifies how you can use those opportunities to engage with your teams. However, none of the tools are intended to be fixed to one stage or scenario. Table 0.1 in the Introduction shows how the tools might work in different scenarios or how they might work together to complement each other.

In the coming sections the importance and business impact of good employee engagement will be highlighted. But the overall ethos of this book is to introduce some simple tools that are time and cost effective, and can contribute to delivering engagement among your workforce. There is no one single fix for employee engagement – it is not in any one single tool, but in mixing and matching according to your business needs, culture, size, etc (see Table 0.1 in the Introduction).

I mentioned earlier that these were tools, activities and exercises that I have experienced, borrowed, gathered, tweaked and created. In most cases, my research has not identified a specific person or organization to whom to attribute the development of any of these tools to (there are a few exceptions), but I do want to be transparent that these are not all original ideas – some have been observed, tried, tested and amended, others are adaptions and some are original creations. It is not the intention to claim ownership of any of the individual ideas in this book, and I will be pleased to acknowledge the copyright of any material if this is known.

By bringing these various tools and activities together in one place, by making them accessible to all at work, and by providing some suggestions on evaluation, I hope to enable and inspire managers throughout a variety of organizations to engage employees – simply, cheaply but effectively.

The structure of the tools

The book is organized in sections that highlight the need to – and some approaches to – engage employees at each stage of the employment life cycle, and also to support certain key activities on the business agenda. However this is a guideline – and you should look to use the range of tools as you see fit for your business.

Description

Each tool has a short description that explains in summary what it is and when it could be useful. This is intended to headline the tool for the reader and to provide some context as to how it might be used.

Best for

Each tool comes with recommendations about the audience with whom it is best used – but this too is a guideline. Don't be restricted by the suggestions, though – treat them as recommendations and not rules. You know your people, your teams and your managers so consciously consider, before you go ahead, whether the described activity would resonate with them and have a meaningful impact.

Best when

Each tool also comes with a recommendation about when it might be appropriately used. Again, this should be considered as a guideline not a fixed rule, but considering some of the other things happening in your business at the time will be worthwhile. To get the most from the tools you really need the timing, atmosphere and levels of commitment to be strong.

Resources

Most of these tools can be delivered in-house, by you. You don't always need external support and you should have the information here to help you to prepare, run and evaluate each intervention. For many of the tools, the cost is minimal. In some cases the experience can be enhanced with a small budget, but there are many tools in this book that don't require a financial budget. In some cases, spending some money can add to the quality of materials, or the surroundings of the event, but these are not conditions, rather just enhancements.

Process

The process described should give you a step-by-step guide as to how to utilize the tool. You can, of course, 'tweak' the process to fit your own needs, but stay true to the principle that the overriding purpose for each tool is to engage your employees. Be careful not to make adjustments that limit or remove the opportunities for your employees – even if that is not your intention. Consider any process points from their perspective.

Read the hints and tips before you kick off the process – you might find some useful additions or adaptations to the process.

Hints and tips

The hints and tips are adjustments or additions to the process that you might find useful. They do not fundamentally change the process but there may be ideas and suggestions to simplify, speed up, get more detail, manage different size groups, or suggestions that might require more time or more budget. However, none of these are essential to the running of the tool – don't consider them as barriers. They are only intended as suggestions. The process will run effectively using simply the process as described.

Evaluation

There is little point in utilizing these tools – or any other approaches that you have considered – if you do not pay attention to evaluating the effectiveness of your chosen method. If you don't evaluate or review, how do you know whether you are engaging your people or – in the worst case scenario – finding quite the opposite: that your actions are disengaging them?

To this end you will find some guidelines at the end of each tool on how to evaluate the impact it has had. These evaluations range from a typical happy sheet (did participants enjoy the event – see Table 16.2 at the end of this book) through to a deeper evaluation, assessing the impact of the intervention on your key business metrics, not just your people measures. In some tools we provide some great questions to ask. In others we provide a template for evaluation. And some of the tools are useful in evaluating the effectiveness of other tools, and these are highlighted too.

Taking action based on your evaluation is the important part of the evaluation process. If it worked do it more, and find ways to make it even better. If it didn't work, do it less, or do it differently.

Templates and examples

Some of the tools provide you with templates and samples too, so please feel free to use these if they work in your organization or to adapt them so that they can work for you.

Quick view

If you don't have time to read every tool, just turn to the Quick View table at the end of the book (Table 16.1), which provides a clear and fast way to decide which tool fits your engagement needs.

Introduction

What is employee engagement?

Before getting started with these tools with a view to improving or optimizing employee engagement, it is important to reflect on what engagement is, and why it matters. This book is not intended to be a detailed exploration of employee engagement, however, and for an in-depth insight you might consider reading Emma Bridger's 2014 book *Employee Engagement*, which explores in more detail the definitions, importance and implementation of engagement strategies.

However, to fully understand what you are aiming for in your organization – how you might 'sell' it to your leaders, colleagues, influencers and employees – it is useful to have a quick refresher on the key points about what we mean by employee engagement and why it is important in business.

Employee engagement has been defined as 'a workplace approach designed to ensure that employees are committed to their organization's goals and values, motivated to contribute to organizational success, and are able at the same time to enhance their own sense of well-being' (MacLeod and Clarke, 2009). A factsheet on employee engagement by the Chartered Institute of Personnel and Development (CIPD, 2015) suggests that there are three main dimensions:

- Intellectual engagement: thinking about the job or the organization and how to improve it.

- Affective engagement: feeling positive about the job or the organization.

- Social engagement: the opportunity to interact with others at work, and to collaborate on improvements and changes.

It may be that in some individuals, roles or organizations all three are highly visible, accessible and important to jobholders. For others, it could be less so – with one taking priority over others. Throughout this book, there are tools and activities that span the three dimensions and aim to deliver increased levels of engagement, whatever the individual or organization definition of it may be.

In an article for Workspan, Werhane and Royal (2009) state that organizations focus too heavily on trying to motivate employees through financial reward and recognition, an approach they describe as 'risky'. They suggest instead that the focus should be on increasing engagement and providing systems that better support employees for success, which they refer to as 'enablement'.

This connection between engaging employees – connecting them into the overall success of the organization, and enabling them – and ensuring they have the skills and resources necessary to do the job effectively are key to getting employees to perform at their very best. They are multiplicative – one without the other is not sufficient.

Why does it matter?

In MacLeod and Clarke's (2009) major report on employee engagement, commissioned by the UK government, they were able to report on several important research studies that provided evidence of the positive impacts of employee engagement for business success. They reported that increasing employee engagement correlates with improving performance, and quoted research by Gallup, Towers Perrin and from within organizations themselves that suggest that higher levels of employee engagement can result in fewer accidents, less employee turnover, higher customer advocacy, greater productivity and increased profitability, as well as more creativity and innovation than is typically seen in those companies with lower engagement scores. In addition, they report the positive impacts of engagement on measures such as sickness absence and company pride, and Leary-Joyce (2004) adds that positive engagement and a great company culture will also lead to easier recruitment and better staff retention.

Bridger (2014) concluded that engaged employees perform better, work harder and smarter, give more discretionary effort and offer greater competitive advantage than those who are disengaged. It therefore suggests a sound business case and a solid return on investment to commit to actions that encourage the engagement of employees.

A fully engaged team means that everyone contributes equally to the overall success of the team. For the individuals who make up those teams, who on average will spend around 30 per cent of their lives at work, it is surely better to enjoy what we do, to feel a connection to it and a sense of purpose, and to feel good about the team, surroundings and environment we work in.

Leading engagement

As a manager, one of the first things to consider when thinking about your role in engaging your team is just how engaged you are yourself. If you are to be a credible leader and to influence your team to commit, to go the extra mile and to really align behind the goals of the organization, then you really need to be doing those things yourself, properly, before you start.

There are a few questions you should ask yourself to test your own level of engagement:

1 Do you know and understand how your job connects to the overall goals of the business... and does that connection interest and excite you?

2 Are you willing, and able, to take full accountability for your work?

3 Do you feel stretched and challenged by your work? Are you always willing to take on bigger challenges?

4 Are you an advocate for the organization and its work?

5 Are you motivated by – and receiving – positive feedback from stakeholders that matter?

Do you know why it matters?

Knowing and understanding why employee engagement is important will help you to put the right focus on it, but also to understand how it can be achieved. I have provided a high-level overview of what engagement really is. You need to be comfortable with that but, more importantly, know why it is significant.

There is evidence described in the previous section that demonstrates the business benefits of employee engagement, and it is hard to imagine a business that doesn't want to achieve these things – increased productivity, easier recruitment, employee retention, improved customer service, etc. Paying lip service to engagement is quickly uncovered by employees; they can see through words to a lack of action very easily – but real, meaningful engagement could make a significant difference to your business success and your employee well-being.

Influencing engagement

At the top

If you are a senior leader in your organization, you need to set the standard and act as a role model for employee engagement. Working with your senior peers, you have the power to set the tone for how the organization works, and to determine the prioritization for employee engagement in your business goals or your objectives. Employee engagement will need at least one advocate, a representative at the highest level in the organization who can promote the connections between the organization's business deliverables – both quantitative and qualitative – and the well-being, the motivation, the resilience and the involvement of its employees. I encourage you to let that person be you. Be the spokesperson on your senior leadership team and promote employee engagement as an enabler for improved organizational performance.

With peers

Whatever level you sit at in your business, you can be an influencer. You can influence your peers to take the employee engagement challenge seriously, and to work with you to spread some great examples of engagement initiatives across the organization. This is particularly important where cross-functional approaches are used, building collaboration, sharing knowledge and collectively problem solving. To be effective, employees in all of the functions involved should be looking up to a leader who is an advocate, and who understands the 'what' and the 'why' of engagement. Share your book, share your ideas, and work with your peer group to encourage a range of tools to be adopted across your organization.

Bottom up

You do not have to be in charge to set the tone and the standards in your own part of the business. You don't even have to be a team leader or a supervisor. Many of the tools in this book require little time, and little budget, and most can be done where you work, some of them literally where you work – at your desk, in your open plan office, etc. By using such accessible tools, there is the opportunity to try some out, to work with your own colleagues and make suggestions to your line manager about tools or interventions you could use to stimulate some thinking, to get some new ideas, to welcome new starters, or to support those leaving the organization. You can start small fires: try out some 'safe' or gentle tools and techniques, and see if they work – talk about and advocate them if they do, and watch them spread in usage across the broader organization.

Building skills

Knowing what you have to do is only part of the story. Knowing how to do it is often harder. Developing the skills for delivering employee engagement can be difficult – there are so many definitions of what it is, and so many ways that you can encourage or enable it. Within this set of tools, I have tried to provide many that require little specialist skill. There are some, but not many, where facilitation skills, for example, may be a prerequisite. The intent is that with the guidance provided, and enough preparation and time for proper consideration, you should be able to pick up many of these tools and use them.

However, ensuring that you are sufficiently 'enabled' is an important part of making the use of tools effective, so more than just reading the tools it is useful to understand a few other factors too:

- Organizationally:
  - What is the organization's approach or attitude towards employee engagement? Are they typically advocates of such initiatives, or against them?
  - Has anything similar been done anywhere else in the organization?
  - Is there anything else going on in the organization that might impact engagement activities (ie downsizing, acquisitions, uncertainty, major customer issues, etc)?
  - Are there any experts or specialists in your organization who might be useful to you – ie human resource (HR) specialists, engagement specialists, facilitators (including scrum masters) etc?

- As far as engagement goes:
  - Do you understand enough about employee engagement, what it means and how you might enable employees to feel engaged?
  - Do you know how the tool you are planning to use contributes towards greater levels of engagement?
  - Does the organization have any preferred approaches for engagement? Does it measure engagement?

- Your own capabilities:
  - Have you had previous experience of facilitating, or leading a meeting or a workshop? If not, have you considered getting some top tips from those who have?
  - Are you confident in your capability to facilitate, not dominate, the team environment? What skills should you be adding to your portfolio? How will you handle those who challenge you or the process – or both?
  - Do you have two or three great coaching questions up your sleeve to encourage open discussion? Try these – questions like these will not be appropriate for every tool, but the common approach is to stay open-minded and ask, not tell:
    - What else could we do? What else? And what else?
    - What are others doing? What else have you seen? What else have you experienced?
    - If there were no barriers what would we do?
- Your team:
  - Are they mentally ready for the experience you are about to offer them? Or are they distracted with other priorities?
  - Is the timing right?
  - Are they open to new ideas, new thinking?
  - Do they believe that you genuinely want to get their inputs?

Engaging people

Expectations of your employees

There are many theories we can read that tell us about what motivates people to come to work, or memes that we see on social media to remind us, or we can assume that we just know – people are motivated by financial reward and recognition, personal challenge, security, etc. Whilst I would not be critical of such theories, I would argue that they are generic. They provide a framework from which we can consider motivational theory, but what is of more interest is what happens in your own organization. The theories will become significantly more valuable if you can you personalise them so that they relate to your type of business, to the culture you have, to the environment you operate in, or to the individual needs of the types of people or even to the individuals that your organization employs.

It is not always easy to know, understand or recognize what your employees are looking for to encourage them towards higher levels of employee engagement. To add to the complexity, your organization is made up of a group (or maybe multiple groups) of individuals, each bringing their own preferences, needs, motivations and desires into the workplace. One size will not fit all – there is no one answer to how to increase employee engagement, as different people will react differently to your activities, ideas and exercises.

As a starting point, the simple solution is just to ask people what motivates them. Managers and HR professionals are often not comfortable asking such a simple question – based on the principle that they are running the team/department/function/business – and should probably know! However, by asking people (be it individuals or groups) what motivates them, what might make them connect to the organization and its goals, you can – where practical – rethink your ways of working, your interventions and initiatives to their needs. You will find some tools in this book that might help you to do that (consider using dialogue sheets for example) – to reach out to your employees and seek their input.

Consider the simplicity of asking the question from the employee perspective too: your manager is sufficiently interested in you – and how s/he can help you to stay motivated – that they asked you what you need in order to do so. You do, of course, have to be prepared for the responses that relate to more money, longer holidays, bigger bonuses, less work, etc. However, if to avoid such responses you don't ask the question, then you limit your opportunity to get some real and rich information about motivation factors in your organization. Some typical questions you might like to ask could include:

- What does a 'great day' involve for you?
- What gives you the best sense of achievement?
- What is important for you to enable you to work at your best?
- How do you prefer to be managed?
- How do you like to be recognized or rewarded?

Focusing on these questions may encourage responses away from the danger zones mentioned above, but they may not. Financial and security aspects may be critical motivators for some employees. The key message here is that it may not be for everyone. Be inquisitive, don't be judgemental, and use the responses you get in order to be flexible in your approach to encouraging engagement.

Opportunities to engage the people in your organization, at all levels, can present themselves in a variety of ways and at different times. In this book, I start with the idea that you can engage people on an individual, team or organizational level and I have identified tools for each of those scenarios. It supports the concept that you can start small if that feels appropriate, and work with individuals to gain commitment, or you can work with a whole organization (depending on the size and practicalities, of course) on a common initiative.

Engaging one-on-one

The tools in this section are targeted at engaging on an individual basis with your team members. They outline some opportunities and some of the needs that employees may have, and some approaches to how you might be able to encourage engagement through those.

Engaging teams

Tools described in this section are typically focused on teams that are interacting or working together regularly. Whist some might be relevant and appropriate for a larger audience, it is not always practical, but adapting the tools may be effective for bigger groups.

Engaging the organization

These are tools that can be used to impact across the whole organization, whether involving everyone at the same time, or in stages, or whether it is the outcomes that can be used to encourage engagement.

Engaging through the employee life cycle

Throughout an employee's career, they move through various stages, from starter to leaver. The life cycle may well stretch for the full career span with one employer (from apprenticeship to retirement) or may repeat over time with different employers. Regardless of that path, it is highly likely that through that career span, other things will happen. There may be promotions; transfer to a different business unit, function or geographical location; career or specialism changes; or, from a personal perspective, there can be life changes that impact on career, such as becoming a parent, a change in marital status or a long-term illness. We call this journey the 'employee life cycle'.

This book is structured in a way that highlights the need and the opportunity for engagement at every step of that employee life cycle, starting even before a new starter applies for a job, and continuing through to retirement. At each stage, tools are applied that may be unique to that situation, or could be used in a variety of scenarios, but there are continuous opportunities to build and sustain engagement throughout an employee's employment with you, and these should be optimized.

The following sections explain why it is important to engage at each stage in the life cycle:

In talent attraction

Any candidate for a job in your organization – from initial applicant to final – stage interviewee – is a potential employee. To add to this perspective, in modern-day recruitment activities, social media plays a large part in the recruitment and selection processes, with candidates (unsuccessful or otherwise) more than willing to share through social media their experiences of your company, your people and your interview processes.

In addition, competition for top talent is high, and you want to beat your competitors to the best. Keeping high-calibre people engaged throughout the process – however long – will be critical to ensuring that you are able to pick from the best candidates.

How you set the tone in your recruitment processes will be important in not only attracting and retaining the best talent, but also in making advocates of all candidates who experience your recruitment campaigns. This means that several things have to be considered, from how you brief external agencies, to the communication and level of feedback you provide at every stage, the information you give about your organization and the quality of your representatives through the recruitment process.

In induction

An article by Fulham (2016) quotes research carried out by YouGov, which found that 19 per cent of new starters were actively looking for a new role, and 30 per cent plan to leave their job in the first 12 months. Could this be attributed to either a poor recruitment process or a poor induction? Focusing on the engagement of new employees will help you to establish a sound base for their future career.

Induction can be a confusing period for new employee – filled with optimism and excitement, but also with nerves, discomfort and frustration. The new employee is likely to want to be able to get on with the job, to add value and build relationships quickly. Formal induction processes can slow that down. Giving consideration to how to engage employees as early as possible in their career with you, and seeking to make the induction process more engaging, will help commitment and retention, as well as setting the tone about how your business likes to treat its employees.

In training

Training provides a great opportunity to stimulate engagement in employees. Training delegates are often a captive audience, but they can be reluctant learners on occasion too, sent to training to fulfil a quota or compliance to corporate requirement. There are opportunities to optimize their engagement in the learning experience, however. The tools provided relate to learning focused on informality, short sessions, and practical and collaborative learning from the experiences of others. These are not intended to replace formal classroom learning, on-the-job development, e-learning or any other training method, but to complement them and provide more opportunities for those keen to learn and develop.

When life-changes happen

For some employees life changes – for example having or adopting a baby, illness, family bereavement or other life-changing events – may require or lead to an extended period of agreed leave from work. It is during these periods of extended absence that an employee can easily disengage from work. There may be some situations where this is advisable (work-related stress, for example) but there may be others where continued engagement and contact with an employer is beneficial. From a company perspective it can only be advantageous, reminding the employee that they are missed, keeping them in touch with what is happening in the business so that they are up to date when they do return, and maintaining some of the social connections that can be important to individuals. Most importantly, retaining the connection with work during an extended absence is likely to make the employee feel valued and involved – even if remotely and even if only occasionally. The tools related to this section are intended to focus on the positive aspects of keeping engagement high – it is not the intention to address absence issues through the use of such tools.

When career changes happen

When employees face career changes that might see them move around or up the hierarchy, we often forget the importance of induction. Providing the newly appointed internal employee with the opportunity to re-establish themselves in the organization in a new role and/or a new team – maybe even a new location – can be a critical part of their re-engagement process.

On leaving

It may seem counter-intuitive to spend time engaging those who have already chosen to leave your organization. However, if you are facing a 'regrettable loss' – ie a leaver who you wish would stay – you should consider the benefits of keeping them engaged until their point of exit. Remember again that a leaver is a potential advocate for your organization – to its customers and to potential future employees but also to current employees.

In addition, consider the personal engagement that you might feel if the company continued to seek your input, involvement, ideas, etc, even though you are leaving – a very different approach to not bothering to ask.

And, of course, you do want to encourage a positive handover and knowledge sharing prior to the exit. Keeping your leaver engaged is likely to make them more willing to do this effectively.

Also, as a regrettable loss, you may hope that the employee considers returning to your business one day. A positive experience during their last few weeks or months with you is much more likely to make that a possibility.

On retirement

Of course a retiree is also a leaver but in some cases they may well deserve special treatment and here that is what we assume. The retiree may well have been in your organization for some time, and those who have usually leave the company with a great deal of experience, knowledge about the business, legacy and skill. Keeping them engaged as they approach retirement can help to ensure that they are able to continue to add value, are seen as valuable (by you and their colleagues) and they may even be able to add a few new skills to their portfolio before they leave. As one manager once told me: 'We just let them wind down and slip away quietly at the end of their working life.' Whilst this may be appropriate for some we should not assume that it is right for everyone. We should make an effort with those retirees who still have more to give.

Engaging in the business

In the same way as we should give serious consideration to each stage of the employee life cycle, so we should also give serious consideration to each stage of the business cycle. It is easy to anticipate that certain generic 'events' will happen during an employee's tenure with your organization, and these too provide opportunities to engage that should be optimized.

Whether the business is just ticking along, allowing the opportunity for simple everyday engagement, or whether there is a need for improvement (to service, quality, efficiency, etc) or change (reshaping the business, changing product lines, etc), or it may be that you want to put additional focus on customers or suppliers, or on the delivery of business results – each of these scenarios is a platform to launch or continue employee engagement, and the following provide more information about those opportunities.

One of the key principles of this book is that engagement is not a one-off initiative. It is not a project to focus some attention on only until you have it. This is not something that HR has to do – or even wants to do – for you, though they will support you. It is an ongoing process – a continual effort to ensure that people in your organization feel engaged with your business.

The tools in this book should help you along the way, and particularly with the conscious effort you may need to make in order to get started. But ultimately it must become 'just the way we work around here'. You may find ways to use the tools that work best for you: things that you want to do regularly, other tools that work on occasion, and probably some that don't or would not work for you at all.

As a line manager, this needs to become part of your way of working. You need to be engaging employees every day.

Engaging for business improvement

Whether your business needs a complete turnaround or just a continuous effort on improving its product, service, quality or cost, engaging your employees in the process will help you to get commitment to implementing and delivering new ways of working. There are tools in this book that can bring employees into the improvement process at any stage, be it identification of an issue or opportunity, development of new ideas, creative solutions or cost-reducing initiatives. Their involvement can bring a different perspective, providing ideas that are influenced by their experience of doing the job, handling the product, interacting with customers, etc – and that experience can be invaluable in rethinking how things can be done.

In addition, involvement at an early stage is more likely to secure commitment to making it happen. Employees who have been involved in designing processes are likely to be more invested in implementation, in demonstrating that their ideas can work, and that their involvement was worthwhile.

Engaging in change

Organizations go through change all the time, whether it is the implementation of a new system, or a complete overhaul of product or process. Whilst the common view is that people don't like change, a more considered view is that people don't like having change done *to* them. When change is inevitable, people want to be informed and, wherever possible, involved. Much like with the improvement challenges, employees who are involved in change are more likely to advocate and support it. It is therefore valuable to spend time helping people to understand what the change is, and how they might react to it, ensuring that they fully understand the changes that are happening and getting them involved in the process wherever possible.

Customer focus

Whilst we may be in contact with customers or suppliers on a regular basis (in some organizations maybe daily, if not more), we do not take the opportunity to really engage with them as often, if at all. Engaging the customer or supplier can bring many advantages – the opportunity to understand their needs better, the opportunity for you to explain your needs, seeing how things can be improved or why things might be going wrong. This interaction – though it needs to be carefully managed – provides the opportunity for more dialogue, for collaboration and for ongoing improvement. For the employee, there is the opportunity to meet the customer, to gain a deeper understanding of how they can help and to improve service, quality, cost etc. Their involvement in these types of activities – the opportunity to spend time with the customer or supplier, involvement in ideas and changes, and the ability to be part of making it happen, and evaluating it – are all factors that positively impact on employee engagement.

Engaging in delivering results

One of the common success factors for organizations that feature in the best companies or 'great places to work' lists is that people know and understand their jobs and how what they do every day makes a contribution to the overall goals and aims of the company. Engaging people in what has to be delivered at organizational, functional, team and individual levels allows them to have a line of sight from their day-to-day job to a meaningful outcome. Further enabling people to consider how they could do their job better, faster, more collaboratively, etc, may be more engaging still.

Don't forget the small stuff

Whilst the tools in this book are a great resource, it is important that you don't forget the 'small stuff' – the little things that you can do every day to support engagement activities within your team. Here are a few ideas – but again the list is not exhaustive. Consider what it is that matters to you, and add that to your own personal list of the small stuff you must not forget:

- 'Good morning'/'Goodnight' – a simple greeting at the start or the end of the day goes a long way to building relationships with your team. We have all had a boss who didn't say good morning when they arrived… and we probably didn't like it!

- Bring in the treats occasionally for no reason at all – and yes, pay for it out of your own money, don't expense it! You will be surprised at how far a box of doughnuts can take you in goodwill.

- Join your team for lunch every now and again – don't always be too busy, or mixing with a management crowd. Break down some barriers by inviting yourself along and engaging in lunchtime chat.

- Make time for informal meetings and conversations – individually and collectively. Don't save everything for the formal sessions – when you can, and if it is appropriate, share news or announcements in a less formal setting.

- Break out of the office occasionally. Being trapped behind your desk all day will not give you the opportunity to get to know your team members, or to know what is really going on in the team. Get out there and mingle.

- Stop e-mailing, and start chatting. Get out from behind a screen and go and personally discuss issues or challenges or updates with people beyond your team.

- Be fair and consistent in your dealings with employees – nothing puts people off more than unfair or unjust recognition or reward. Bear this in mind when you are reviewing performance, celebrating success or publicizing someone's extra efforts. Don't avoid the difficult conversations with one employee, because it may lead to several more difficult ones coming your way later on.

Selecting the right tool

It is not as simple as 'one size fits all'. In selecting tools to use for your teams you need to consider your objective, their objectives, their current level of engagement, what they like and enjoy doing, and how far out of their comfort zone you want to nudge them. Many of the tools in this book are adaptable – and I encourage you to consider them as flexible, so that you can ensure that the tool or tools that you use meet your specific needs.

In addition, whilst the tools are categorized into the sections previously described, many of them will cross over into other sections too – whilst some are targeted at individuals, for example, they could work equally well with a team.

And finally, some of the tools can work well together. This is mentioned in the tools themselves, but some additional thoughts are included in Table 0.1. This table shows the 50 tools and identifies the appropriate audience for each (individual, team or organization) and whether any other tools might complement or support them. Use this as a guide – it is not exhaustive, but consider your audience and your objective, and make your own connections if you wish to.

Table 0.1 Selecting the right tool

	Engaging one on one	Engaging teams	Engaging the organization	Combine it with
Analogies		•		
Artistry		•	•	
Back to the floor		•	•	Columnist
Benchmarking roadtrip	•			Commitment cards
Birthday breakfast	•			
Celebrating career	•		•	Connecting lessons
Change champions			•	
Chew and chat		•		Mood board
Clear objectives	•	•		Making connections
Columnist			•	Back to the floor Standup
Commitment cards	•			Making connections Customer experience
Common cause			•	
Communicate, communicate, communicate		•	•	
Communities of practice		•	•	Connecting lessons
Compelling brand		•		
Connecting lessons				
Customer experience	•			

Media training		Top team unplugged
Mentoring	•	
		Light bites
		Chew and chat
Mood boards	•	•
Peer post	•	Farewell letter
Pinspiration board		
Preparing for change (P4C)	•	Light bites
Progress bar	•	Making connections
		Common cause
Re-enable	•	Enablement
Re-engage	•	
Shadowing the customer	•	
Stand-up		
Marketplace		•
Roadshow	•	•
Top team representative		Change champions
		Standup
	•	Columnist
Top team unplugged		Media training

Engaging one on one

1 Find a friend

Whilst the development of good working relationships can happen naturally through the course of our work – after all, many of us do spend most of our time working – there are things that you can do to create an environment that provides opportunity develop professional and social connections, and encourage them to flourish.

Employee surveys have reported that having a friend in the workplace is a key factor to employee engagement and whilst it is not necessarily the responsibility of the employee to 'create' those social relationships, you can create the climate and opportunity that enables it to happen more easily.

Presented here are a number of ways to encourage those connections. Be careful that you are not trying to 'force' people into friendships. By creating the opportunity and the right environment it can happen naturally.

Best when

This is an ongoing initiative. Creating the right environment is not a one-off initiative and should not be reserved for new starters to your team or business.

Best for

Your focus may well be on creating opportunities for new starters or transferees into your team, but this should not be at the exclusion of others, nor should it be bespoke to that specific scenario. Ongoing activities will allow relationships to build throughout all levels and functions of your organizations.

Resources

The resource requirements or investment you need to make will be dependent on the initiatives that you undertake. However, none of these need to be at high cost and so funding should not be a barrier. The most significant investment is likely to be time – to establish, communicate and run activities, and for people to participate if you allow it in work time.

Volunteers to organize events or co-ordinate activities will be extremely beneficial. Identifying people who have an interest in doing so will get things off the ground quicker.

Outcomes

These initiatives will ensure that the environment that people work in is a sociable one, and one that provides opportunity for new friendships. This in turn provides an internal support network for employees and it may provide opportunities for stress relief and downtime, as well as some fun in the workplace... in turn, this enables greater levels of engagement.

Process

1 Induction buddying. Don't attach your new starters to just one person. Provide them with the opportunity to meet a variety of new people in their first few weeks – mix it up across different teams, functions and reporting lines to ensure a diverse range of people are introduced to each other. Include transferees, not just new starters, in the induction buddying process.

2 Establish a social committee made up of volunteers among the teams or the whole company. Encourage them to plan events, activities, outings, etc, but be clear about time and costs – will you allow any activities to take place during work time, or are all activities to be done in social time only? Is the company willing to subsidize any social committee-recommended activities, or all they all at the employees' own costs? Make sure new starters/transferees know how to get involved.

3 Get involved in theme days. There are various 'theme days' that crop up across the calendar such as Comic or Sports Relief, Christmas Jumper Day, International Women's Day, etc, and encouraging your team's involvement in them can feel like bringing a bit of fun into work. Consider how you would get involved, or create your own themes as the company takes on a new customer or a new region (eg if you bring on board a client from the United States, make that your theme for the day that the customer comes on board). Consider big events such as World Cup contests, the Eurovision Song Contest, etc – and how you could use those to support your social activity agenda.

4 Create a social space. In trendy start-up and creative agencies they may provide table-tennis tables, football tables, PlayStation, etc. You may choose to do this, but what you really need to deliver is a space for an informal drink and a chat.

5 Use social media. Set up group pages for employees and employee/company interests.

Hints and tips

- Bear in mind any policies you may have about workplace relationships and potential conflicts of interest that might arise. Be transparent about the potential impacts of people's relationships with others at work – including issues such as the fine line between building relationships and potential harassment – but don't highlight these in such a way that it puts people off.

- Make sure you have a clear social media policy in place. Employees need to understand what is and is not acceptable on social media and any consequences of not complying.

- Consider whether you need to set any expectations related to relationships at work. When planning your activities, think about different preferences people have. Not everyone will feel comfortable in large groups; for others, one-to-one interactions or finding their own connections may be further out of their comfort zone. Presenting a variety of options will be more likely to find an approach for everyone.

- Encourage the social committee to adopt the 'common cause' tool (Section 3) for some charitable or community initiatives.

- Relax a bit. Worrying about employees spending too much time away from their desks will hinder your find-a-friend strategies. Focus on supporting the positives of these initiatives, rather than on creating firm rules and policies for the few who may take advantage. Manage them as the exception, rather than the expectation.

Your social media policy should include

- Clarity on what your organization considers to be acceptable personal social media use, if any.

- Clarity about how employees can utilize business social media – your company Twitter name, hashtags, Facebook pages and LinkedIn profiles. In the best examples, companies will encourage a clear delineation between personal social media and company social media – suggesting that an employee may be free to post whatever they wish, provided their profile is not connected in any way to the company profile or brand.

- Defining what would be considered as unacceptable and prohibited use of social media.

- Explanations of how you will monitor your employees' use of social media and personal e-mail.

- Descriptions of how you will deal with inappropriate use (which may include reference to the disciplinary policy).

Evaluation

The evaluation of these initiatives will vary dependent on the activity that you decide to undertake, and the investment that the company makes in financial, time and resource commitment. As an overall guide, you want to know that people are enjoying their work environment, are making connections with others, and that those connections are enabling people to create friendships where they choose to do so.

You can ask simple 'pulse check' questions to find out if people consider work to be fun, if they have a friend at work and if they enjoy social activities at work. This will give a high-level indication of their satisfaction with your initiatives, but establishing the link to employee engagement itself is harder.

2   Peer post

The results of many opinion surveys show that one of the simple things that employees say they crave is a simple 'Thank you'. Whilst as a leader you do have a role to play in recognizing the efforts and outcomes of others, it is not exclusively your job. You can do much to encourage everyone in your organization to do just that, and through 'peer post' you can provide both the opportunity and the tool. You provide simple postcards and empower all employees in your organization to informally send one with a personalized note to their colleagues, peers, bosses, etc, when they have been helpful, supportive, customer-focused, innovative – anything that promotes positive behaviours in your organization.

It is engaging because most people do not go to work solely to earn money. Most want to do a good day's work and be recognized and praised for doing so. Peers are more likely to notice and appreciate the smaller added-value things that their colleagues do that support others – and the very nature of peer feedback and recognition means that it feels more genuine and 'in the moment' than feedback or thanks from a manager, which has a tendency to feel formal and appraisal-like. Additionally, research in the United States (Novak, 2016) found that 76 per cent of people keep handwritten notes, which makes the peer post approach more impactful and meaningful than sending an e-mail or a passing thanks in the corridor.

Best when

Peer post is an effective way of building an informal and very low-cost recognition approach into the way your organization works. It presents opportunities to promote and recognize efforts to collaborate and work effectively across teams to deliver against goals, targets and day-to-day working demands.

Best for

Peer post is intended to be an effective recognition tool for all employees. It is targeted at peer-to-peer collaborations, but this should not exclude using it for manager-to-employee – or vice-versa – recognition. Encouraging a broad use of this approach across your organization will only mean that more people are getting recognized for something that someone valued in their work, and that can only be a good thing.

Resources

Whilst not expensive, investing a bit of money into simple but effective and professional-looking postcards will be worthwhile. This can be achieved relatively cheaply, but you will need to have a supply of cards across all your working locations so that employees have easy access to them as and when they want to send one. Reduce the cost and complexity by sticking to a couple of standard designs on each print run, but changing them frequently will be important (see 'Hints and tips', below). This is not a time-heavy initiative – preparing and printing the cards is a simple task, but communicating the approach may take some time to embed.

Outcomes

The primary intended outcome of a peer post initiative is that employees feel that discretionary effort and collaboration are recognized by their peers. However, there are other beneficial outcomes. Organizations may experience an acceleration in discretionary effort – knowing that it is valued and appreciated by others may make employees do more of the same, or start doing it if they see others being recognized. Additionally, as colleagues begin to recognize each other's efforts, so teamwork and opportunities for collaboration increase. Silos may begin to break down, particularly if cross-functional recognition is promoted. Teams will begin to understand how they can positively impact on the work of others further down the process chain.

Process

1 Communicate about the peer post initiative and its purpose and intent. Make sure people know the criteria for sending a card (ie if you feel someone has helped you, supported an activity, gone the extra mile for a customer) and encourage people to participate. Don't be too prescriptive though – allow people to thank others for what was important to them, not what *you* think matters.

2 Provide cards, make them visible with supporting promotional material (posters, etc) and keep them topped up so that they are always available for sending.

3 Encourage recipients to pin their received cards around their workspace – this is a visible indication that the process is effective, and highlights

clearly who is receiving them. The more people see it being used for recognition, the more likely they are to send one.

4 As the manager – notice! Engage with team members who have received a card, talk to them about what they did and support the recognition effort. Provide your own feedback too.

Hints and tips

- Don't judge who is getting what. With peer post, you are allowing people the freedom to send a card to anyone they wish to, based on something that they think was done well or was particularly helpful. You may get a few that don't meet your own criteria for that, but empowering others to recognize colleagues means you have to allow them to do it their own way. You should only consider intervening if the recognition is sent for a behaviour or action that is counter to your values or goals.

- You may want to refresh the design or messaging every few months – it keeps interest in them alive and may encourage further recognition. If an employee has to send the same card twice it might not have the same impact for either the sender or the receiver. Updated designs will mean that your team members can collect from a range of postcards if they continue to perform in ways that their peers appreciate.

- Keep the language on the front of your postcards relevant to your audience. A young group might prefer a 'cheers dude' whilst an older employee base might get more connection with a traditional 'thank you'.

Evaluation

The primary – and perhaps most simple – measure for peer post relates to how many cards are being sent. Keep track of how many are available, at the start and end of a review period (monthly is probably most realistic), and assume that the delta is the number that have been sent.

By engaging with people who have received them, you will also get a sense of the recipients, and the actions they are taking to prompt the recognition. In specific cases, this may warrant further recognition, or you may want to highlight to the wider organization the kinds of behaviours or actions that are leading to peer post cards.

You may also get a sense of who the most frequent senders are – and consequently who is not sending them. You may not want to consider or address this on an individual level, but if you know that certain departments are not participating, you can look to address this.

3 Letter from the top

As the leader of your business, or your team, how often do you put pen to paper to recognize the efforts of a team member or colleague? This tool recommends that you do just that – a reminder to use one of the simplest engagement tools available to you: to write a letter or note of thanks. It's a great tool to use when you want to react immediately to an individual's performance, and you want to recognize it with more than just a passing thank you.

Best when

An individual in your team, another team or a peer or colleague of yours has gone that extra mile, achieved something unusual or extraordinary, made it through a difficult period or experience, or delivered something that you were not expecting. They may have done something that you have noticed, or that others have noticed and mentioned to you (your customers for example). It is best captured 'in the moment' – as close to the time of the incident or experience happening as possible. Don't procrastinate over it – if it caught your attention, then put pen to paper straight away.

Best for

This is a tool that is not only effective for employees at all levels across your business, but can also be beneficial for contractors and temporary workers, third-party suppliers, or other key stakeholders. Whilst you may not feel it is essential to secure the engagement of those not employed by you, consider whether in doing so you may increase your reputation as an employer, service provider or user of contract services, and think about the benefits that this might bring. For example, your actions may evoke greater commitment and therefore less turnover from temporary employees, which can only be advantageous to your business.

Resources

This is a very low-cost, low-effort approach to recognition and engagement. It uses only the time it takes you to write a note, and the cost of the paper you write it on.

Outcomes

It is intended that the letter from the top brings a smile to the face of the recipient. A very simple approach to recognizing the simplest of acts in day-to-day working life can add to the motivation and engagement of an employee – they know they are doing the right things, and that the things they are doing are noticed by you, by their colleagues or by the customer.

It is engaging because the employee feels recognized and valued.

Process

1 Get a pen, get some paper or a card, and write a letter. Write it in pen, in longhand, yourself – it is much more personal than sending an e-mail, for example, and shows that you have taken some time on it.

2 Personalize the letter as much as possible – at the very least, demonstrate that you know the person you are writing to by using their first name, the one they are known as rather than the formal one that may be recorded on your system.

3 Be as specific as you can about the thing you are recognizing or thanking them for. A general 'you did a good job' will probably still land well, but if you can reference the specifics of what you have seen or experienced, the receiver will be clearer about what they did well, why you liked it and why they should keep on doing it.

4 Sign off the letter informally, but make sure the employee knows who it is from.

5 Give some thought to how to get the letter or card to the recipient. You might want to pass it via the direct line manager, or deliver it yourself. In some circumstances it may be appropriate to put it in the mail (internal or external), but there may be greater impact if it is delivered personally.

Hints and tips

- Having some thank-you cards or notepaper in your drawer in readiness will be an advantage – but just your standard thank-you notes, nothing corporate or branded. This is about you personally sending out a thank you.

- You can use this kind of letter to support and advocate behaviours and actions that you want to see and develop in your business. Highlighting them in the letter will make it easy for people to connect the positive recognition with the specific behaviours or values that your organization advocates.

- Don't overdo it so that these letters become commonplace. Make this a 'special' thing that people talk about, and that they are proud to receive because it is unusual. Don't do it so rarely that your teams don't know about it – but this should be done with an irregular heartbeat. It should not be in your monthly plans, or target-driven. If nothing has happened, no letters. If lots has happened – lots of letters!

- Make sure your direct reports know about this tool – not only should they be providing suggestions to you about letters you could be writing, but they might also want to do the same.

  Of course there will be some cynicism (shaking the envelope waiting for the cash to fall out?) but it will still have an impact.

- Don't just write 'down' your organization – ie to those more junior to you. You should also encourage writing to peers, and maybe even to your bosses!

Evaluation

In employee surveys, asking questions about recognition, being valued for contributions, etc, will give you an indication about how initiatives such as this may be working.

Listen out for the chatter – what are people saying about receiving a letter like this? Where are the letters going – do you see them pinned up in personal desk space, or going in the bin? React to what you see happening.

Is the act of recognizing a behaviour encouraging others to adopt it – are you beginning to see more of similar positive behaviours?

4 # Benchmarking roadtrip

Your employees could well be the best source of new ideas, innovations and process improvements for your business. However, when we focus on the same tasks, within the same environment, we rarely get – or take – the opportunity to see things differently. Sending an employee or two on a roadtrip could deliver some great benefits, as well as improved engagement.

The benchmarking roadtrip suggests that you send out an employee (or two) to test out, look at, and/or experience the ways that other businesses do things. It might be the competition, it might be a comparable industry or sector, or it could be vastly different. Briefing your benchmarkers will be important. They need to be clear about the objective of the experience, and what you expect from them on their return, as well as how it will work practically. In principle, they take a day away from the normal working environment, they take inspiration from others, and bring back some findings, ideas and recommendations.

Best when

This tool is particularly beneficial when you are open to gaining some fresh ideas, insights or opportunities. It works well when you feel that the organization could take and respond to some inspiration from outside. However, be careful of the timing – if there are challenges in the business that are not related to your objective for the benchmarking roadtrip, it could be seen as inappropriate or may lack some credibility as an initiative.

Best for

Employees at all levels across your business can and should participate in the benchmarking roadtrip – don't make this a hierarchical 'entitlement' for managers only. Where possible, encourage participants from an area of work or who undertake a task close to the one that you want to benchmark. The more relatable it is, the better it can be for the participant, and the more likely it is that they will bring back useful ideas.

Resources

This is a very low-cost, low-effort approach to engaging teams in creative thinking and initiating change.

You will need to consider the expenses incurred on a trip – travel, lunch and anything that you may need them to buy to complete the experience.

The time out of the business for the employees is a factor to be considered. Typically this could be a half-day or a full-day experience, but allow enough time for it to be valuable. Don't stick too closely to your own geography just for the sake of time – you may lose an opportunity.

Outcomes

The intention is that, through the employee's experience of benchmarking, the business identifies new ideas, fresh thinking and a bottom-up initiation of change. Seeing how things are done elsewhere should provide fresh perspectives on how tasks can be done, or on product or service offerings, and as a result your benchmarker should return with some inspirational ideas.

It is engaging because the participating employees feel valued and that they have had an opportunity to be heard, and to influence – but only if they come back with ideas. It is not a day off – and it is important to be clear what expectations you have.

Process

1 Talk about the benchmarking trips as an opportunity through your usual communication channels. Take care to describe them well, explaining what you expect from benchmarkers and what they will be required to do.

2 Identify who/what/where to benchmark. A brainstorming session with your managers or board may help to generate some ideas – but consider all of the following questions:

  – Who: which companies make sense, who are your competitors, who are in similar industries?

  – What: which parts of your business or process do you want to focus on – a certain product, a specific process point, a policy or procedure?

  – Where: is it appropriate to look locally, regionally, nationally or internationally?

3 Identify the right employees to send out. You could consider opening this up to all employees to register interest and select some volunteers. Alternatively, ask your managers to provide some handpicked nominations.

4 Provide a brief. Explain clearly what you want benchmarkers to do before the trip, during it and what you are expecting from them on their return. You may need to support them in setting up meetings, or access to other companies.

5 Offer support on benchmarking day. A quick call or message on the day will encourage them, and remind them that they have your support.

6 Provide the opportunity to feedback to yourself and/or a wider group. Having been clear about your expectations before the trip, and explained the output that you want, this should not be a surprise. You should consider whether this is an informal or formal feedback process, in person or in writing.

7 The worst-case scenario is to do nothing as a result of the trip. If there are no actions to take, communicate across the organization what was discovered on the trip, and why you are not taking any action as a result. Ideally you will be able to share some key findings and a few small actions from the benchmarkers' roadtrip that will be taken as a result.

Hints and tips

- Announcing this as a great new initiative will raise expectations that you may not be able to live up to, so keep it low-key and just focus on one trip or objective at a time.

- Don't constrain yourself to your industry – look at what you might be able to take out of some very different industries.

- Providing the opportunity to give feedback is important – but be wary of setting up a formal feedback presentation to a senior team as this may be a part of the process that employees feel most stressed about and it could impact the effectiveness of the process. You could instead ask them how they would like to give feedback – a report, a one-to-one with their manager, or a presentation – playing to their preference might get the best out of them in this scenario.

Evaluation

- How many ideas are your getting? How relevant are they? How many have you implemented?

- What is the take-up rate of volunteers/invitees to take a roadtrip?

- What is the feedback coming back upstream? What are you hearing about the roadtrips?

5   Commitment cards

The commitment card is an A4 piece of card, with a visual image or a short punchy statement on part of it that asks team members to record their commitment to your company goal, their team purpose or to their own individual action plan. The commitment card asks colleagues to write down their commitments, and to display them prominently for you, their teammates and possibly customers to see. You can work with each team member to ensure their commitments are aligned to the overall business or team direction. By simply having them on display you create a talking point, an instant measurement and an ownership from the individual to the commitment they have made, but you also have visibility of the team's commitments or focus areas, and can encourage a clear line of sight between their commitments and the overall goal of the team or the organization.

Best when

The commitment card works well when you have engaged the team in a workshop or meeting and are keen to encourage their commitment in the follow-up. It provides one way of you keeping up momentum, and keeping conversations alive.

Best for

The commitment card is appropriate for all levels and all employees in the organization. It should not be hierarchical – if you are asking your team to put down their commitments, then senior managers should put down theirs too.

Resources

There is minimal time and cost requirement to deliver the commitment card. Cards can be 'home-made' at minimal cost – just printing and card. Whilst you may want to add professional touches (team photographs, professional printing, etc) these are not material to the success or otherwise of the card initiative, but may improve the overall aesthetics. Remember though that the commitments are time bound – so this is not a long-term investment – the commitment card may be updated or renewed and replaced regularly.

The time commitment too is minimal – you will most likely be discussing the commitment during your meeting or event, so the added task is only to confirm, write and post the commitment card.

Outcomes

Leary-Joice (2004) suggests that when people take responsibility they take ownership for success and will feel empowered to deliver their part of that overall success. Completing the commitment card can encourage people to take that ownership.

Process

1 Prepare the commitment card template prior to your meeting or event. Keep it simple by just designing or printing your own card – or if you feel the investment is worth it, involve a design and printing team to get it done professionally. The card should show the vision, an inspirational quote or an engaging image (depending on what is important to you at the time) on one half of the card, with space on the other half for the individual's commitments.

2 At the end of a strategy, team build or objective-setting workshop or meeting, ask team members to write down their commitment(s) – eg how they can support/deliver/contribute – what they commit to do.

3 At the end of the event, collect in all the commitment cards. This safeguards against them getting lost, left in cars or forgotten about. Take some time to review them to familiarize yourself with the commitments your team have made. If you can, before the team arrives the next day, get them pinned up visibly in their office space. They might take up a team noticeboard, or you may be able to get them pinned up in the workspace or desk for each individual. Keep them visible – the cards should stimulate discussion and collaboration, so having them where colleagues can see them and comment on them is an important part of the process.

4 Transfer the commitments to the individual's objectives or performance review – this makes sure that the process is seamless, and the commitment is not seen as an 'extra' but as part of their day job.

5 Make sure you follow up – in walkabouts, managers should take the opportunity to chat about the commitments with employees – how is it going, are they still valid, do they still see the link with the vision? (But be gentle, it is not a test, it's a chat!)

6 Keep them alive, don't allow them to go unnoticed and fall out of date. Encourage people to note updates on them, tick when something is achieved. Treating the commitment card as a live document will add to its value.

7 Renew and refresh the commitment cards at your next event or meeting.

Hints and tips

- Use a photograph of the employee: make them more fun by adding a picture of the person as well as their name – you can add a new and informal talking point that can help to break down barriers if you ask them to attach their baby photo, a caricature, a 'selfie' or a picture of the superhero they would like to be! These small talking points encourage people to interact informally about the commitment card... and that could lead to discussions about the commitment, about how they could help each other, work collaboratively, achieve more together. If you can do it, why not get an informal picture of the whole team to put on there?

- Use an inspirational quote: the internet is a great source for inspirational business quotes. If you want to use one of these on your commitment cards, make it relevant and connected to the goal or the commitment you are looking for. Here are some topic-based examples of quotes you might want to consider:

  - For customer focus: 'Get closer than ever to your customers. So close, in fact, that you tell them what they need well before they realize it themselves.' – Steve Jobs

  - For innovation: 'If you can dream it, you can do it.' – Walt Disney

  - For teamwork: 'Coming together is a beginning; keeping together is progress; working together is success.' – Henry Ford

  - For personal development: 'Continuous effort – not strength or intelligence – is the key to unlocking our potential.' – Winston Churchill.

There are plenty more like this to be found online, so find one that is right for your organization, your culture and your current goals.

- Using imagery can also be quite powerful – if you can use pictures from your business that are relevant to the goal, all the better. Pictures of your products, of services in action, of sites, locations or core activities, and including your logo, will all make the card more relevant and meaningful for team members.

An example:

Figure 1.1

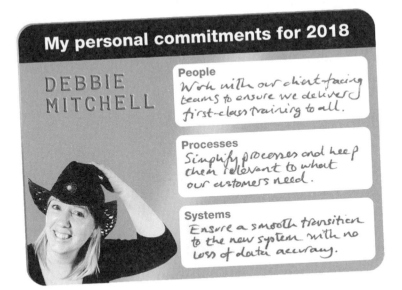

My personal commitments for 2018

DEBBIE MITCHELL

People
Work with our client-facing teams to ensure we deliver first-class training to all.

Processes
Simplify processes and keep them relevant to what our customers need.

Systems
Ensure a smooth transition to the new system with no loss of data accuracy.

Evaluation

The initial evaluation for commitment cards is simply a question of whether each employee has made a commitment, has posted it visibly in the work-space and has been able to deliver against that commitment.

Harder to assess is the degree to which the team is talking about and collaborating on their commitments. You might also consider how much more aware managers are of the commitments of their team.

More indirectly, you may be able to assess whether the delivery against commitments has had any bearing on service levels, productivity, efficiency, sales or profit.

6   Clear objectives

Whilst effective objective setting is a part of any standard line manager's training, its importance for employee engagement is often overlooked. Concerns about a company's appraisal processes, or the effective cascade of objectives, often present opportunities for managers not to set objectives, and concerns about where they come from and how to structure them effectively are often a basis for poor objective setting.

Engagement surveys show that employees want to know what they have to do, they want that to be motivating (although what motivates each one may be different) and they want to know how what they do each day contributes to the overall goal of the organization. With those key engagement factors in mind, the setting of quality objectives becomes extremely important.

This means that you are likely to get the best performance from your employees when they understand the objective, can see its relevance, are motivated by it and have a reasonable chance of achieving it.

Best when

Setting clear objectives is best as an engagement tool at any time that you want to allocate tasks, responsibilities or development opportunities to an employee. There may be an annual performance cycle, and whether your organization's performance review processes are formalized and structured, or informal, you should have some process of determining each employee's contribution to the business goals through individual task or objective setting. Establish whether this is a regular cycle, or whether those objectives are set and reviewed according to the individual's role. Working to the established timeline will allow the opportunity for some structure in the process, and ensure that performance against those objectives is reviewed in a timely manner. However, setting clear objectives is an ongoing task and critical to retaining the engagement of your team members.

Best for

- *All employees*: every employee in the organization, regardless of seniority or function, should have clear objectives against which their performance and contribution can be measured.

- *New starters into your team*: whether they are from outside the organization or internal transfers, new people joining your team should be allocated objectives for their new role. This helps to mark the closure of one set of tasks for internal transferees, and helps the joiner to quickly understand what it is they have to do, and how they will be assessed. It provides new joiners with the opportunity to quickly engage with the team and start to see the impact of their work on the overall team performance.

- *Underperformers*: for those employees in the organization who are not performing, a clear and focused set of objectives that are regularly monitored and reviewed will allow the opportunity for a line manager to manage the performance to an acceptable level (and hopefully above) or to demonstrate a lack of capability to perform in the role (and manage the consequences, having done so).

- *High performers and employees who want to develop*: some employees may be considered to be performing extremely well in their role, and whilst there should be other interventions to ensure that their talent is optimized and retained, the setting of stretching and challenging objectives should not be underestimated in its ability to engage the high performer. In such cases, the more stretching the better, and objectives should provide an opportunity to work cross-functionally, in challenging projects and with different stakeholders or team members. This allows the high performer to raise their visibility and prepares them for potential cross-team transfers or promotion.

- *Leavers and retirees*: it may seem pointless to set objectives for those who are already planning to leave the organization, whether by retirement or resignation. However, it can be extremely useful to consider setting objectives that allow the exiting employee to consider what they want to achieve prior to their own exit (what would they want their legacy to be) and/or to set specific objectives that focus on the closure of activities or projects and the handover of specific tasks.

- *Career breakers*: setting objectives can be a useful tool for maintaining the engagement of those taking a career break, for whatever reason. In some circumstances (not all) it may be beneficial for a manager and employee to work together to establish some objectives for the career break itself (eg keeping in touch, benchmarking other companies whilst travelling, or learning new skills), or objectives that might be implemented on their return to work.

Resources

No specific resources are required, but as preparation material you may want to gather and review some of following documents:

- your company or divisional strategy;
- team goals and targets;
- the employee's job description.

Outcomes

A clear set of objectives can be motivational and engaging for your team members. Ensuring that employees understand what they are being asked to do, and why it is important, encourages that engagement and commitment.

Objectives that set clear expectations allow you to effectively monitor and manage performance. Do not assume this is all negative. Clear objectives mean that you can see where there are shortfalls in performance or delivery. They can also help you to recognize (and therefore reward) when performance is on track or beyond your expectations.

Regular monitoring provides you with the opportunity to address either of the above issues. Where an employee falls short, more focused discussions are needed about progress, actions and where they can improve – this kind of help should encourage them back on track. Where an employee is exceeding your expectations, regular review provides the opportunity to ensure that speed of delivery is not at the cost of the 'how' of performance.

Process

1 Establish the reason for setting the objective. Knowing and understanding this context will help you to frame the conversation with your employee most effectively. Take some time to consider whether the employees is underperforming or overperforming, motivated or demotivated, planning to leave the company, etc.

2 Schedule a meeting to discuss and agree the objectives. Draft out some focus areas where the employee could contribute – ie in projects, initiatives, delivery of tasks, etc. Ask the employee to do the same as pre-work for a meeting. At this stage, they should not be fully formed objectives, but may become so later in the process.

3 During the scheduled meeting, share your ideas, and collaborate to identify an appropriate set of challenging objectives.

Hints and tips

- Meet face to face to discuss each employee's objectives – this task is not engaging or motivating if it is all done by e-mailing back and forth.

- The 'making connections' tool (Section 14) can be an extremely beneficial precursor to the individual objective-setting process. It provides clear line of sight between the overall company goals and the individual, creating the connection between what the employee does and how the company succeeds (or otherwise).

- The copy/paste approach to objective setting is not an effective way to ensure that the team collectively achieves a group of goals. If your own objective is to 'save 10 per cent' then copying that into four sets of employee objectives will not work. You need to ensure that you are able to allocate proportionally and/or give specific and job-relevant tasks; also consider how motivational it would be if your objectives were just a copy/paste from your line manager. You may take the view that they are simply giving you their job to do.

- Does your objective pass the 'stranger' test? If you handed that objective to me would I be able to understand what was expected, and would it seem interesting, exciting and challenging? To pass the stranger test the objective needs to be clear on task and expectations, free of jargon or acronyms, explicit on measurement and with a transparent timeline. Often we assume that people know what is meant by what we write, but giving a few minutes to consider the stranger test will allow you to challenge your own assumptions and provide a great-quality objective.

Evaluation

The evaluation of effective objectives happens at three main levels:

1 The first is to look at the objective and determine whether it meets the basic requirements – that is, is it a SMART* objective, clearly documented, stretching and aligned to the organization's goals? Is it written simply and with clarity – that is, does it pass the 'stranger' test? A simple test of these points is to ask the employee to clarify their understanding of what they are being asked to do.

2 Second, is it engaging and motivational? To achieve its purpose in relation to delivery of task, the objective needs to meet the above criteria. But more than that, if it is to be engaging and motivational, there needs to be

stretch and opportunity to do something new, different, challenging, etc. The employee will be the main judge of that, but bear in mind that you may not find the same things exciting or challenging.

3 Third, has it been achieved? The primary measure of whether an objective was effective is whether it was achieved, and how it was achieved.

4 Finally, consider whether the achievement of this objective contributed to the overall success of the team/function/business.

---

*SMART = Specific, Measurable, Achievable, Realistic and Time-bound.

Engaging teams 02

7　Dialogue sheets

The dialogue sheet, a concept that I understand to have first been introduced by Stockholm KTH University, and later developed by other advocates of the process, is an informal and often unfacilitated process that enables small teams to discuss topical issues, with a view to providing feedback, ideas, insights or opinion. They use a large sheet or 'tablecloth' to prompt and record their discussions.

The concept as introduced by Stockholm, and developed over time by other practitioners, is in essence a simple one. Small groups discuss a specified issue around a table with a tablecloth upon which they can actively note their comments and ideas. The more informal the better for the dialogue sheet, and often it works well with coffee, doughnuts and without an appointed facilitator or manager to guide the discussion. A self-managed group will take the conversation where they want to, prioritizing what they see as important and enabling a wide range of feedback to the originator of the exercise. Different groups are likely to see things differently, so running the session a few times with different sets of participants can provide diversity in feedback.

The 'tablecloth' is often the key for this tool. The tablecloth can be 'populated' or designed by the originator to steer the discussion. Whether creative and imaginative, or just posing key questions or words to evoke discussion, the dialogue will initially be driven by these prompts. This can come down to both your artistic/creative abilities and/or the budget you have to help with those things. However, this works as well with a large roll of paper and a marker pen as it would with graphic design and professional printing – so don't be put off! The critical success factor is in posing the right questions or posting the right prompts, so you will need to think carefully about what you are asking and what you actually want from the exercise.

Best when

The dialogue sheet is a great concept to be used when you want people to engage in proposals, change, or to support implementation of initiatives (eg values, goals, etc). It is most effective in an informal environment, and when not being controlled or managed by someone who is not in the group.

It is possible to run multiple groups at one time, because there is no intervention, so this can be an effective way to manage breakout groups in a larger workshop. Alternatively you can run the dialogue-sheet exercise a number of times in succession, as the outcome is open (no fixed answer or format).

Best for

The dialogue sheet is best for small groups of six to eight people, as the principle requires that there is a lot of self-managed discussion in the process. Larger groups may need more facilitation and you may find that it is more difficult to involve everyone in the debate.

Depending on your subject matter, it works effectively for cross-functional groups, and it does not take account of seniority in the process. However, it is important to make sure that a mixed group is not dominated and/or led by an individual who is more senior.

Resources

You will need a very large sheet of paper – at least A0. If you cannot easily get a sheet that size then just put together four flipchart sheets. An alternative is to buy a paper tablecloth, although you may find the quality is not good for writing on so choose carefully. Ideally this will be printed with your discussion points (see later comments). Provide lots of coloured marker pens for participants to make notes, and some Post-it notes may be useful.

Outcomes

The dialogue sheet should encourage discussion, debate, feedback and commitment or buy-in. Its true output is entirely dependent on the objectives you set, and the questions or statements that you pose on the sheets. However, whatever the topic, in my experience, participants feel engaged by the process, and generally report that they feel they have had an opportunity to share their opinion or shape a debate.

Process

1 Identify four to six statements about the issue/project/change, or select key words from a vision statement or mission that could prompt good discussion (controversial can be good!) and write them in the corners of a large sheet of paper.

2 Invite small groups (around six people) to get coffee and biscuits (promote informality), put the sheet of paper on the table and invite them to discuss, write comments, questions, etc.

3 Minimal intervention from a facilitator allows freedom of discussion and debate within the team.

4 Allow around 30 minutes for discussion – and then give the group a chance to give feedback to a facilitator.

5 Key points should be noted and fed back to key stakeholders.

Hints and tips

- Make this process have the feel of a social occasion. Encourage participants to bring coffee (or provide it in the room) and offer sweets, biscuits or donuts.

- Poster Pigeon offer extremely good value poster sized prints on their basic quality paper – which is perfect for a dialogue sheet. www.posterpigeon. co.uk

- An example of a very simple dialogue sheet is shown on page 44. You will see some company values noted around the sheet and some prompting questions to kick start discussions. Participants can follow any order they wish to in this example and note their discussion directly onto the sheet.

- Alan Kelly's website (as mentioned in the Acknowledgements) contains some great information about how to use the dialogue sheet concept and includes some downloadable examples of dialogue sheets. However, they are somewhat more advanced than my example. You should consider which one you might feel more confident delivering, and which one your participants might feel more confident to use and choose an appropriate template. Or mix the two and design your own. www.allankelly.net/presentations/dialoguesheets.html

Evaluation

Get a view of the level of engagement during the discussion – how much participation is there? Do people seem interested in the subject matter? Are there lots of comments and opinions?

Second, take a view of the quality of the discussion and feedback that you have experienced through the course of the session. Have any of the discussion points impacted your approach? Has the feedback led to any changes or have any of the ideas or suggestions been implemented?

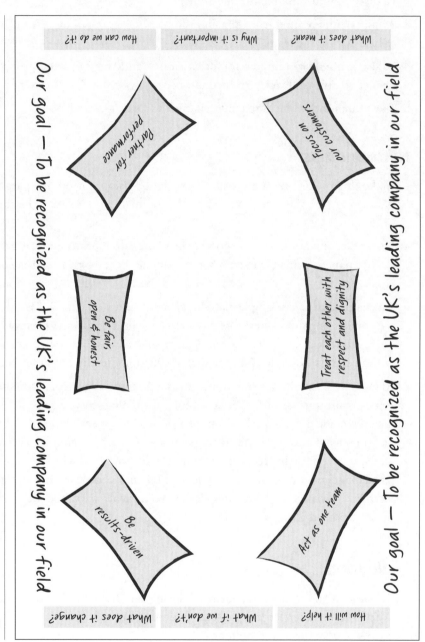

Figure 2.1 Sample dialogue sheet

8   Hot topics

The 'hot topic' session is a short, sharp activity for someone to share a problem or a challenge with the team, and get a set of ideas/solutions/feedback/thoughts from across the breadth of the group. It allows an individual to bring a challenge to the table, for others to understand that challenge, and then generate unlimited ideas for the individual to take away and consider. It enables fast responses, shared learnings and best practices, and maximizes the opportunity to utilize the diversity of the team to generate new thinking.

Best when

Hot topics is a great tool to use when you have a challenge and you want new ideas on how to address or solve the problem. It works most effectively if your issue is clear and simply described – if the issue is ambiguous then the responses could also be vague.

Because the time commitment is limited to 30 minutes, this is an activity that can work well in your normal meeting schedule (you could have a regular 30-minute hot topic session on a monthly management meeting, and invite team members to take it in turns to bring a challenge), or slot it into a normal working day without too much disruption to your routine.

Best for

- Any teams at all – this works well with a group of strangers, or with a well-established team.
- Mixed or diverse teams – invite or encourage participants from different levels, functions, specialities, etc, as this will encourage a broad variety of perspectives and ideas.

Resources

This is a process with a fixed and rigid duration – it will take 30 minutes. The only costs incurred are for Post-it notes, pens and attendee time.

You will need a room, ideally a space where your participants can stand, move around and work at a flipchart, OR a space where you can gather around a desk or workspace and share ideas, etc.

Outcomes

At the end of this activity, the participants will have offered a variety of solutions to the problem owner. Typically, participants offer between three and six Post-it ideas each (although their input is unrestricted so it could be many more than that) and with a group of five participants the owner could have up to 30 suggestions to take into consideration. The thinking styles and ideas will vary and that means that the owner may have access to suggestions that s/he would not otherwise have considered.

It is engaging because individuals remain accountable for their own decision making. How they solve the problem remains theirs throughout – but by offering a range of solutions, you can encourage a different approach. Participants value the opportunity to be part of a solution, and to be heard.

Process

1 The 'owner' needs to identify the problem or challenge before starting the activity – and should have given some thought to how to present it in a short summary.

2 The owner should briefly outline the process, and their expectations of the participants – eg the context of the issue, what will happen to the outputs and how participants should contribute (eg be creative, be honest, be constructive, have fun with it).

3 The owner introduces the topic, providing some context and a summary of the problem or challenge (five minutes).

4 Participants then take the time to ask clarifying questions – this is not an opportunity to start 'solutionizing', though – be strict and ensure that the questions are to clarify understanding of the problem or challenge (five minutes).

5 Participants work individually to note down ideas, challenges, feedback, etc on Post-it notes – one idea per Post-it. Remember that the intention is to be supportive and offer help, new ideas and fresh thinking – don't be critical – be constructive (five minutes).

6 One by one the participants put their Post-it notes on a board/flipchart – explain their suggestions in brief to the owner. If something has already been covered, offer the Post-it but without going into explanations. The owner should offer no reaction at this stage, but can ask clarifying questions if necessary. At the end of the 10 minutes, the owner should have a

good number of Post-its in their possession with varying ideas related to their challenge (10 minutes).

7 The owner provides a closing summary of their takeaways from the process – identifying suggestions that may have particularly resonated, or been totally new thinking. No judgement is offered on the ideas – instead the owner takes away everything that has been offered by participants in order to give the ideas due consideration, and later decides on a course of action (five minutes).

8 The session closes.

Hints and tips

- Stick rigidly to the timing in this activity – this is all about a targeted and focused set of responses to a challenge. Whilst that may limit the number of Post-its that a participant can feed into the process, they do have awareness of the issue and can always be encouraged to follow up afterwards if they have further contributions to make.

- Ensure that the problem owner is open to ideas and feedback. They are encouraged not to respond to the Post-its in order to demonstrate an open attitude to the contributions from others. Allowing the opportunity to comment could lead to defensive or negative behaviours. Encouraging them to stay neutral during the feedback process, and open to considering every idea on the Post-its, will ensure they get maximum benefit from this process.

- Watch out for 'sensitive' challenges being tabled in a non-confidential environment or with an inappropriate group of participants. You may need to postpone the session, or ensure that all participants recognize the confidential or sensitive nature of the topic.

Evaluation

- How many ideas were generated around the table?
- Was one of the ideas implemented (either in entirety or in part)?
- What are people saying about the process – do they find it useful? Act on that feedback!

9   High-performing teams

The characteristics and behaviours demonstrated by 'high-performing' teams are well documented, but this activity is designed to encourage your teams to think about what is most relevant for THEM to be able to operate in a high-performing way.

It provides some outline as to what a high-performing team typically does, collated from research and theories on the subject, but encourages the team to take a practical and collaborative approach to determine their own criteria and to establish a charter that they can all sign up to.

By not dictating what the team should do, or how they should behave, you encourage the group to define their own ways of working, and to prioritize what is important for them. This may change over time – this exercise can (or should) be repeated, as the different challenges the team faces, or the different levels of maturity of the team, may impact what it takes for them to perform at their best.

> 'The way a team plays as a whole determines its success. You may have the greatest bunch of individual stars in the world, but if they don't play together, the club won't be worth a dime.'
>
> *Babe Ruth*

Best when

This works best when the team is reasonably well established and either wants or needs to improve its effectiveness. It can be useful in the early stages of team development, but it is important that the team members are able to be open and honest with each other throughout the activity. Whilst the focus is on how the team works, there may be some challenging feedback and all team members, and team leaders, will need to be open to hearing it, and taking action on it.

Best for

This exercise can work effectively with any teams of around six to ten people who are looking for ways to collectively improve their ways of working and collaborating with each other. This is not restricted to any hierarchy within the organization, or for any size of business. The important factor is that most of the flash cards used in this exercise are relevant and relatable for the team, and they are empowered to make changes to how they work, based on the outcome of the exercise.

The full team should be involved in the exercise, including the team leader or manager of the team. Any absentees might be concerned that they were not involved and therefore not buy into the new ways of working.

Resources

This activity could take anything from 30 minutes to half a day, depending on the number of steps of the process you want to follow.

This is a zero-cost activity – you just need to allow for the participants' time. The materials required can be prepared in advance, using card and flipcharts. You will need:

- a room – ideally a space where participants can stand, move around and work at a flipchart, or a space where you can gather around a desk or workspace and share ideas, etc;
- flipchart paper;
- coloured flipchart pens;
- high-performing team cards (see 'Materials' for recommended content);
- charter template (see Tables 2.1 and 2.2 below, under 'Materials' for recommended content).

Outcomes

At the end of this activity, the team will have agreed on the characteristics that could build them into a high-performing team, and will have identified a concise action plan that can help them to achieve it.

It is engaging because you are providing the team with the opportunity to set their own standards and priorities for how they work together – having that level of empowerment in how we work keeps us engaged in the team development process much more effectively than being told how to operate or what we should do more of.

Process

1 Brief the team on the purpose of the activity – for them to identify what could make them a higher-performing team, and to establish what they are willing to do collaboratively to achieve that.

2 Provide the team with the high-performing team cards and ask them to sort them into an order of importance for their own team. Ensure that they know to keep it relevant for the team, for what is important for them right now. Recognize that it could change later, but that given their current status, workload, challenges, etc, the top priorities will be those that can help them to address challenges and achieve goals together. Provide some blank cards, so that they can add any characteristics that they feel are not represented on the cards provided.

3 There is no fixed definition of the terms used – and allowing the team to collectively determine any that might seem ambiguous will allow them to reach a shared understanding – so allow them to discover it for themselves, and if necessary respond to their challenges by asking them what it means for their team. The team may also see some of the cards as similar in meaning, in which case encourage them to either group and rename the cards that they see as connected, or to remove one of them (their choice as to which is removed from the list).

4 There needs to be a consensus of opinion to really make this work – to achieve that might call for some longer discussions and debate, but ultimately they need to agree on their top five or six. There is no strict limit to the number in top priority but it is important to keep it realistic and manageable – a maximum of five or six should be achievable.

5 Transfer the prioritized team characteristics onto the measurement chart template – this will allow you to identify where the team is today and where it wants to get to. Asking each participant to plot current and desired state onto a chart will give you a holistic picture of the team's self-assessment, and an idea of the gap to be addressed.

6 Ask the team to work through their prioritized characteristics and complete the team charter template – identifying one action that they can all commit to for each characteristic that will help them to close that gap.

7 Once they have all agreed, encourage them to sign the charter and agree a date for review.

Hints and tips

- The charter should be kept as a live document – it will change as the team evolves and the team members should be encouraged to review it regularly, to reprioritize the characteristics as things change and to consider the progress they have made since the first gap analysis.

- The team characteristics cards are offered as source of material, but you might want to add your own or take some out, depending on your team.

- The team charter is also provided as an indicative template – please do adapt it so that it is relevant and practical for your team to use.

Materials

Create the high-performing team cards using the following characteristics. Add your own suggestions too, and leave some blank for participants to add their own suggestions:

- Involvement
- Shared success
- Support
- Creative
- Trust
- Common goal
- Build self-esteem
- Alignment
- Manage conflict
- everyone contributes
- Clear decision making

- Clear team roles
- Ambitious goals
- Shared accountability
- Clear purpose
- Team processes
- Mix of skills
- Task-focused
- Communicative
- Innovative
- Enjoyment
- Competitive

- One voice
- Commitment
- Healthy debate
- Constructive feedback
- Strong leader
- Compliant
- Passion
- Inspire each other
- Results-focus
- Enthusiasm

Figure 2.2 How to complete a team charter

What the team should write

Team characteristic	To us it means...	How we rate today	It is important because...	What we must do
Write in the five or six priority characteristics – each one on a separate row	Ask the team to define what it means for them, to ensure a shared understanding	Ask the team to rate where they are today on the scale between L (Low) and H (High)	Ask the team to say why it's important, in order to get a shared sense of purpose	Ask the team to identify one action they could take to improve their performance in this area

Example

Team characteristic	To us it means...	How we rate today	It is important because...	What we must do
Clear roles and responsibilities	that each person understands what role they play in the team	L ○○○○✗○○○○○ H	we need to be clear about who is doing what in order to avoid duplication	AH to present suggested team roles and response at the next meeting with clear allocations to each team member

Figure 2.3 Sample team charter

Team characteristic	To us it means…	How we rate today	It is important because…	What we must do
		L ○○○○○○ H		
		L ○○○○○○○○ H		
		L ○○○○○○ H		
		L ○○○○○○○○○○ H		
		L ○○○○ H		

Evaluation

Regularly review the charter, the progress made and any adjustments you may want to make.

Review the levels of performance on the measurement chart every three months, using the same process – this will indicate the degree of movement made and any additional actions that might need to be implemented.

10 Analogies

The 'analogies' exercise is a simple and fun activity that allows you and your team to think about what the future might look like. It invites participants to describe the company or the team in different terms – encouraging an open and honest evaluation of the current state and a creative and fresh view of a desired future state. It engages employees by giving them an opportunity to have a say about current issues and to contribute their thoughts about a future vision.

Best when

This can be an effective tool in a number of scenarios – it has been used in setting or securing buy-in to company direction or goals, or when considering or planning a change in the organization. In these scenarios it can help the participants to consider what the future might look like for the organization.

Also it can be used as part of a 'self-assessment' of a team to stimulate change, giving team members a 'safe' mechanism to constructively critique the team, and to position a preferred state. Similarly, it could be used for a product or process review.

Best for

This exercise works effectively for groups of three or more employees, but it is flexible enough that you can use it for a large group, by splitting them into smaller groups to do the same activity, and comparing outputs.

Any level of employee can engage in this activity, but you may need to set the context differently and think about the appropriateness or relevance of your analogies for more senior leaders.

Resources

The analogies exercise will take around 30–45 minutes, depending on group size and the context of the activity. It may be that you choose to do this as part of a bigger workshop, in which case the time required can be adapted to suit your needs.

This is a zero-cost activity. You just need the time, a pen, some paper and some active minds. You don't need a meeting room for this activity, but ideally a space where participants can stand, move around and work at a flipchart. You will also need to have some flipchart paper and pens for each group.

Outcomes

This activity should produce a set of descriptors or characteristics that capture how the company or team is seen 'today' and how it could be seen in the future. It helps to provide a 'from–to' analysis that describes how the company or team could be, and begins to identify the gap that has to be covered if the desired future is to be achieved.

It is engaging because it involves the participants in a definition of what the company's future might look like.

Process

1   Introduce the activity by explaining the purpose, objectives and outcomes you are hoping to see – it is important that people can relate the task to its use, so try to make that connection for the participants.

2   Ask the participants to consider: 'If this company were a car, what car would it be today, and why?'

3   Ask the participants to discuss and flipchart their answers, providing bullet points that explain their thinking and relate back to the company.

4   Allow time for participants to complete this activity – usually around 10–15 minutes.

5   Now ask the same question again, but thinking about it *in the future*: 'What car would this company be, and why?'

6   Ask the participants to discuss and flipchart their answers, providing bullet points that explain their thinking and relate back to the company – this usually takes around 10 minutes.

7   Now ask the participants to give feedback, explaining their rationale.

8   Capture key points on a flipchart as follows: as the team describes some of the characteristics of the car you would be today, capture them in relation to the company on the chart under the heading 'from'; as the team describes the car of the future, capture those characteristics under the heading 'to'.

9   You now have a view of where your team thinks the company should be headed and some characteristics that the company might want to have in the future.

10 Explain how you will use the responses provided and what happens next.

Hints and tips

- Reiterate to your team that it doesn't have to be about moving from a 'clapped-out old banger' to being a 'high performance elite sports car' – you might want to focus on stability, reliability, on customer service, on quality, etc – which might lead you to something less visually attractive, but representing the important characteristics.

- Think about using some of the following analogies:
  - if we were a car;
  - ... an animal;
  - ... a city;
  - ... a cartoon character;
  - ... a country;
  - ... a gadget;
  - ... a chocolate bar;
  - ... a drink;
  - ... a competitor.

- Sometimes, it can be thought-provoking to run the exercise using a couple of different analogies and consolidating the results.

- To make it interesting, print off some pictures of the category you are using for your analogy – and ask the participants to discuss and select one for both NOW and FUTURE.

- Take care not to 'lose' the outputs. Engaging people in an activity such as this but without using or actioning their outputs can be very disengaging.

Evaluation

- How participative were employees in the process?
- How clear is the vision for the future?
- After implementation of change, look back at the outputs you had – how does the new reality compare to the descriptors derived from this exercise?

11 Idea wall

The 'idea wall' activity is designed to engage employees in the creative process, brainstorming and developing ideas and suggestions. It uses a visible office wall space so that ideas are out in the open, and the wall can be added to over time.

Best when

This exercise works effectively when you want to bring together a small group of employees to brainstorm and develop ideas and suggestions for improvements, changes or innovation. This might be during a change programme, for example, where you might want to use it to develop knowledge and understanding of the vision, or the reason for change. You might consider using it to develop new ways of working, reinventing processes, etc. It is an effective tool for problem solving – posing a challenge and seeking new ideas or solutions to overcome it.

The activity is evolutionary – whilst the majority will be completed in one session it can be added to over time. This means that it is accessible for participants to join in.

It provides the opportunity for your teams to be engaged with proposed changes from the early stages by contributing to the first round of suggestions.

Best for

This tool can be used for employees of all levels of seniority, and across all functions, and may be most effective when it involves a cross-section of people from your organization. A mix of experiences, functional specialities, knowledge of your business as well as others (previous employers, for example) will all add to the richness of the ideas being generated.

Resources

This is a zero-cost activity. You just need the time, a pen, some paper and some active minds. The idea wall should be created in the normal working area of the office, using a blank wall or a very large whiteboard. Post-it notes and pens will be needed to capture ideas. The wall needs to remain in place for a period of time (probably around a week, but not too long that people fail to notice it) so that it can be seen, reviewed, noted and enhanced.

The initial session can be a short brainstorming exercise (around 30–45 minutes). Over time, the wall can be added to as new ideas from participants or passers-by are generated from the initial wall content.

Whilst the resource requirement for the wall itself is small, you will need to bear in mind that ideas generated may require some financial commitment to either develop, generate or implement. If financial constraints are such that no budget at all will be available, you should make that clear in your scoping discussion at the start of the exercise.

Outcomes

This activity should leave you with a highly visible range of ideas, suggestions and recommendations from your employees. Some common themes of suggestions may be identified – and this may help you to prioritize some actions – the more people who suggest something, the more priority you may want to give it. It is engaging because employees will feel that they were able to contribute their ideas and suggestions to your challenge.

Process

1 Before starting the session, spend some time preparing a clear question that you want to pose for the idea wall.

2 Introduce the activity by explaining what you want to do, and why you want to do it this way. Talk upfront about how you will use the outcomes of the process, so that people understand why they are contributing, and tell them what you expect from them.

3 Ask the participants your question. Explain the context and any other background information that you think may be relevant – but be careful not to limit the scope.

4 Give participant a set of blank cards (or Post-it notes) and ask them to write down their ideas – one per card. It is not a discussion at this time – it is just their own ideas on a card. Keep the process going until people have started to run out of ideas.

5 Ask participants to post their ideas one by one on the wall, describing the idea as they post it. There should not be any challenge, only points of clarification.

6 Ideas may spark other ideas for other participants, so allow them the opportunity to add to the collection of others.

7 See if you are able to group some of the ideas into common themes – circle those with a marker pen and give them a heading. Be careful not to oversimplify by grouping together too many things.

8 Discuss and agree prioritization of the ideas – or agree a consensus on the 'big three' priorities. One way to do this is to give everyone a sticker (one coloured dot or similar) and ask them to put it against their top priority. Those with the most dots will become your priorities.

9 Having identified the priorities, explain what will happen next.

Hints and tips

- The bigger the wall space, the more opportunity people have to post ideas.

- Keep the wall alive – don't take it all down once you have finished: leave it up for people to add new ideas over a few days and provide different coloured card so that it is easy to see where the new ideas pop up.

- Encouraging people to write things down before talking about them should allow everyone a chance to have a go.

- Do something with it! The visible wall space and activity is highly engaging, unless you don't take any actions or follow up on the ideas presented – make sure it is a worthwhile process.

Evaluation

- How many ideas are generated?

- How many suggestions are followed up?

- What impact are those ideas having?

- Are there other ideas added to the boards after the main event?

12 Mood boards

The mood board is a very simple measurement tool that uses a small number of key questions to gain anonymous opinion and trends. The mood board is usually limited to a series of around three questions, and asks employees to place an anonymous dot/sticker/mark to respond to the questions posed. By doing so, you are able to get a very quick and indicative response to the questions you asked. This can work for you as a speedy opinion survey or feedback tool.

Best when

The mood board is a quick and simple tool to use when you want to do a 'temperature check' of opinion among a group of employees.

It can also be useful for measuring the degree of opinion movement at the start and end of a process or a meeting. By asking for contributions to the same question at the start and the close, you can see quickly whether the meeting or session has been effective or not. It is effective if you are not concerned about specific feedback from named individuals, but rather you are keen to establish a collective opinion or trend at a macro level.

Best for

This is a tool that can work well for employees at all levels across your business, and can include any contractors and temporary workers who may be working in your teams at the time.

Resources

This activity takes just a few minutes, depending on the number of people you are seeking contributions from. You need to allow enough time for people to consider their response – and in large groups it can take a few additional minutes for all participants to complete the task – but this is a short, sharp measure that gives immediate and highly visible answers.

You will need good, clear questions with clear, easy-to-understand rating scales, a flipchart and some stickers or dots for each participant. Ideally, you will have pre-printed sheets with your questions and response scales on, or prepared flipcharts if you do not have the budget or a preference for professional printing. You will need to provide sticky dots or some other form of marker for each participant to be able to add their response.

Outcomes

This activity will provide you with a collective view or opinion set from a team or group of people. It can be used to measure the strength of feeling on an issue, or as a short and instant opinion survey or engagement survey, if you ask the right question. You might also use it to measure a shift in perception or opinion.

It is engaging because participants have the opportunity to have their say, but in a non-confrontational way – and the anonymity it can provide can feel safe for some employees.

Process

1 Consider your question, and the types of responses that you might want (the nature, scale, multiple choice options, etc). Keep the language simple but, in order to avoid confusion, make clear the differentiation between the potential ratings.

2 Write each question on a chart and provide the scoring/rating scale.

3 Provide each participant with one sticker per question, and ask them to respond to the question by placing the sticker at the appropriate place on the scale.

4 Review, with the group if practical, or individually. In general discussion talk about:

   – The clusters of stickers: what are they telling you in response to the questions you asked?

   – The outliers: without making anyone uncomfortable, or highlighting who thinks very differently, you might ask more generally: 'How or why might someone see things so differently?' Put yourself in their shoes for a while, and consider what may have led an individual to provide such a different response to the rest of the group.

   – So what? What does this suggest you have done well, or that you need to do differently in the future?

Hints and tips

- Some examples of questions that work well for the mood-board activity include:
  - 'I understand the company strategy and goals' (measured at the start and then at the end of a communications session), using a rating scale of: Not at all → Partially → Fully.
  - 'How effectively is the team operating today?' (measured during a team meeting or event), using a rating scale of Not at all → Okay → Brilliantly.
- If you are asking a large group to participate, then prepare extra flip-charts with your question on and allow participants to use any one of the boards.
- Provide just enough stickers or dots for each person to have one response per question asked.
- Make it fun by providing silly stickers instead of dots (animals, cartoon characters, etc).

Evaluation

Did the process give you some meaningful results? What will you do with them?

Figure 2.4 Example of a mood board

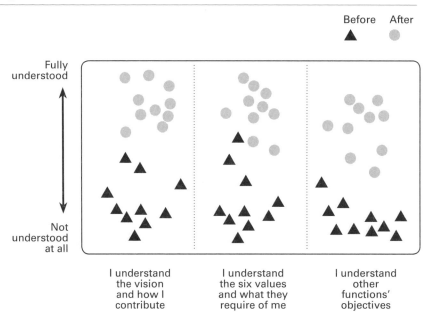

13 Progress bar

You might remember the old-style appeals on UK television that typically featured a thermometer-style tracker, or you may have seen the progress charts for fundraising campaigns that indicated a starting point, key milestones and an end target. As the appeal progressed the thermometer was marked to indicate the progress being made. More recently you will be able to imagine the progress bar on your PC as it loads a new programme or page, or the progress percentage on your Facebook page that tells you how complete your profile is. These visual reminders keep people informed about progress and what still has to be achieved. The progress-bar tool follows the same process. Using a large visual of a thermometer, mountain or wall, or progress bar, clearly displayed in team areas, staff restaurants or reception areas (preferably non-customer-facing) can provide a constant update on progress towards some specific and clearly defined targets or metrics.

As people we are driven to have goals, and to accomplish them. Knowing the progress we are making is important for the latter. There is also a suggestion that without feedback on our progress, we are not able to make meaningful decisions about how we should continue trying to achieve the goals. So the visibility of the progress bar is key to enabling us to make the right decisions about how to achieve our goals.

Best when

The progress bar works effectively if you have a clear and specific quantifiable target to meet that all of a team, function or organization should be able to contribute to and should be engaged in. It is most effective when progress towards the goal is expected to be steady. Seeing little movement towards the target, or periods of inactivity – planned or otherwise – could be disengaging and demotivating, and may suggest that the target is forgotten, irrelevant, out of date or unachievable. Employees will want to see regular updates showing achievement towards the goal.

Best for

All employees will find the progress bar easy to understand to assess progress made and the distance yet to be travelled. However, the level of detail is unlikely to be sufficient for more senior stakeholders and additional reporting will most likely be required.

Resources

Getting your imagery graphically designed and professionally printed will always look better, probably be more resilient and more effective, but be aware of the irony of an expensive (or perceived as expensive) piece of promotional material that is focused on communicating cost savings. Your message will be quickly diluted and lose impact.

You will need to consider naming a responsible person to regularly update the information, so whilst not significant the time for this to take place should be taken into account when planning the process.

Outcomes

You will be keeping people informed of progress, and that can mean they are more engaged in the process. The simple visibility of the progress towards targets – perhaps seen daily if it is in the right place – may encourage greater commitment to it and you may see more push when you are falling behind, or, as you get close to achievement, that final dash to the finish line.

Process

1 As part of a project or initiative you are likely to have targets or goals to be achieved. Identify these targets and break them down into key milestones or chunks that, when achieved, will allow progress to be seen.

2 Design your progress bar to show the measurement and progress. It may be thermometer-style, bricks in a wall or something bespoke or specific to your own target. The progress bar is likely to be a design challenge, so seeking professional help to ensure that it has a professional and impactful presentation is recommended.

3 Identify one person accountable for updating the information against target and agree and implement a regular time/day/date that it will be updated.

4 Once the target is achieved, remove the progress bar and communicate the success story.

Hints and tips

- Don't only use the thermometer for goals with negative connotations (eg efficiencies and cost savings). Focus on some positives such as customer satisfaction, sales, new accounts, net promoter scores, etc).

- Make sure it is kept up to date – make someone responsible for a daily or weekly review and update, and ensure it is done.

- Add a whiteboard or graffiti wall to the thermometer display and encourage people to make comments about significant events, factors or people that have given the cause a push, or make suggestions about initiatives to help reach the target.

- Keep it highly visible and attractive or interesting – add stickers, rosettes or banners, etc, when progress is made or milestones are reached.

- Keep it alive, relevant and meaningful by referring to it in all your project communications and team briefings.

Evaluation

The progress bar is primarily intended to keep people informed, and so a simple evaluation of its success is to establish whether people have seen the bar, and whether they know about the target, the progress and the work still to be done. These are simple questions that can be asked informally at team briefings or in general conversation.

At the next level of engagement, it is interesting to establish how employees feel about the progress being made, and whether they believe there is more that the organization or team could be doing to deliver it faster, more effectively or differently.

14   Communicate, communicate, communicate

A CIPD factsheet on employee communication (CIPD, 2016b) states that: 'Effective internal communication is important for developing trust within an organization and is shown to have significant impact on employee engagement, organizational culture and, ultimately, productivity. Yet CIPD research suggests that many employees feel they receive limited or very little information.'

This last comment from the CIPD is the rationale for referring to this tool as 'communicate, communicate, communicate'. It can be the case that, although you have shared information with your employees, the message hasn't landed, or hasn't been delivered effectively or consistently. Alongside no communication, this miscommunication can be demotivating and disengaging for employees. This tool approaches communications from the same perspective as any other organization, but reiterates that once you have shared some information with your employees, tell them again, and when you think they have got it, tell them one more time.

The recommendation is to develop a standard communications plan, detailing the objectives, audience and key messages for both regular and ad hoc communications activity. However, the process enhancement is in the detail of how you plan and record your reiterations of, and then latterly confirm, the messages conveyed. This should not mean a reinvention of the communications materials, merely that they are presented in a different format or via a different media but to the same audience.

Best when

Your communications plan should be an ongoing part of running your business. It is recommended that you prepare an annual communications plan that provides a regular heartbeat of communications to your employees (including media such as newsletters, team briefings and annual company meetings). The communications plan should be an ever-changing document, however, that evolves with unplanned or unforeseen company news (eg acquisitions, downsizing, relocation, changes to customer base or products/services, staff changes, to name but a few).

Best for

Your communications plan should cover all employees, at every level across your business. The communications plan encourages you to consider the different needs of the audience groups, however – whether that be by seniority, by function, by product line or customer segment. Tailoring one core message so that the different impacts for different audience groups is clear will be an effective and engaging way to communicate across teams.

Resources

Your basic communication plan does not require any resources. You will need to allocate time to prepare communications messages and materials, and you will need to consider the time required for people to attend meetings and briefings. In some circumstances, you may need to use audiovisual (AV) equipment (anything from a simple PowerPoint to a professional AV set-up), and you may use some budget to consider alternative methods of communication (eg videos, off-site meetings, etc). However, financial constraints should never be used as a reason not to communicate with your employees. At its simplest form, communication is just people talking to each other, and is free.

Outcomes

As mentioned in the CIPD quote above, effective communication with your employees can build trust, lead to greater levels of engagement and may encourage improved productivity. By taking the three-pronged approach to delivering your messages, you increase the chances of employees connecting with your messaging, and interpreting what it means for them.

Process

1 Prepare a rolling annual communications plan (you may find helpful as a starting point the template in Table 2.1). Include in the annual plan all of the regular communications activities that you already utilize, such as newsletters, team briefings, annual message from the boss, etc. You may not be able to specify the key messages for all of your annual communications, but complete what you can in the initial draft and continue to update it regularly, adding information as it becomes available or apparent.

2 As you continue to regularly update, include in the plan any ad hoc issues that need to be communicated – these might include key performance indicator (KPI) metrics and results updates, major company news, staff changes, etc.

3 For each of the communications milestones, consider not just the primary communication approach, but also the approach that you would recommend for the reiteration of and the later confirmation of the key messages. Consider using different media where appropriate, and if necessary update the messaging – this may be required if the news, the timing or the stakeholders have changed since the initial messages. The reiteration and confirmation messages should follow within a reasonable timeline of the original, but that may depend on the message, its impact and other business imperatives.

4 Implement the plan, and regularly review and update it as required by changes in the business, stakeholders and the messaging.

Hints and tips

- Utilizing different media across three communications stages may play to individuals' differences and preferences. Some employees may prefer to listen to and discuss new information, whilst others may prefer to read and absorb in their own time. By offering the same information in different formats, messages are more likely to be absorbed by all.

- Encouraging all your senior leaders to take responsibility for communications activities across the business will help to raise their profile and make them accessible across the breadth of the organization. Additionally, the different styles of your leaders may be appreciated by audiences across the business, and their different (although aligned) perspectives on the messaging may create additional interest.

Sample materials

Table 2.1 Sample communications plan

Milestone	Scheduled Date	Objective	Communicate (1) Audience	Key Messages	Media	Owner	Communicate (2)	Communicate (3)
What is the rationale for comms at this time (eg event, activity or monthly scheduling)	*Approx date*	*What is the objective of this comms activity – what are you hoping to achieve by communicating*	*Who is the target audience – this may be split for each comms milestone or objective*	*What key messages are you trying to convey through this comms activity – try to keep to a small number of key messages (3–5 max)*	*How will you communicate?*	*Who is responsible for making it happen? This person may not be required to develop content or deliver but has overall accountability.*	*How will you reiterate what you have told them?*	*How will you finally confirm these messages?*
Monthly team briefing	15 Jan	Update on company progress – sales, new customers and key metrics. Keep employees informed	All employees	Sales are up by 15% thanks to great efforts across the teams. Onboarded two new customers in the last quarter – we lost one due to cost issues in our bid	**Team briefings** No powerpoint. Use prompt sheets only. Record any FAQs	DM	**Email** to all – include any slides used	Make slides available on intranet site or noticeboards – e-mail to confirm that they are accessible

Project implementation	1 Feb	Announcement of new system go live Inform on training plans, and new ways of working Get employees' input to the roll-out process	System users	New system go live Changes Training plans What it means for your daily routine	Group **workshops**	AB	Follow-up in the team briefing	Send e-mail
Project implementation	1 Feb	Announcement of new system go live Keep employees informed	All other employees	New system go live Impacts system users May see slowdown in response times during early stages of implementation	E-mail	DC	Reference to e-mail in the next team briefing	Send text on go live date

(continued)

Table 2.1 (*Continued*)

Milestone	Scheduled Date	Communicate (1) Objective	Audience	Key Messages	Media	Owner	Communicate (2)	Communicate (3)
Monthly team briefing	15 Feb	Update on company progress – sales, new customers and key metrics Keep employees informed	All employees	tbd	Team briefings No powerpoint Use prompt sheets only Record any FAQs	DM	E-mail to all – include any slides used	Make slides available on intranet site or noticeboards – e-mail to confirm that they are accessible
Monthly team briefing	15 Mar	Update on company progress – sales, new customers and key metrics Keep employees informed	All employees	tbd	Team briefings No powerpoint Use prompt sheets only Record any FAQs	DM	E-mail to all – include any slides used	Make slides available on intranet site or noticeboards – e-mail to confirm that they are accessible

Etc

Table 2.2 Media choices

Media	Great For	Watch Out For
E-mail	• Fast, consistent messages where you need clarity in writing • Can be stored for records	• Its one way – you may not get feedback, messages could be misinterpreted – or lost • Can be forwarded
Text/WhatsApp, etc	• Short, sharp messages, preferably just good ones	• Seen as informal; sending any serious or bad news by text or social media is to be avoided
Phone call	• One-to-one interactions	• No eye contact or visual cues or clues during the meeting – you can't judge people's reactions or interpretations
Teleconference	• Bringing together remote workers or virtual teams without the need for travel • A quick virtual round-table catch-up	• The quality of the meeting may depend on the quality of your teleconferencing set-up • Meetings can happen within meetings that are difficult to keep up with remotely • No eye contact or visual cues or clues during the meeting – you cannot judge people's reactions or interpretations
Web meeting/conference	• Bringing together remote workers or virtual teams without the need for travel • Slide-based presentations	• Technical difficulties – often delay the start of meetings as people try to log in at the last minute
One-to-one, face-to-face meeting	• Difficult or sensitive conversations that may impact individuals differently	• Making sure that you convey the same messages to people where necessary
Team briefing	• Sharing updates and information	• The post-meeting meeting at the water cooler – encourage team members to be open in the meeting
Workshop	• Involving others in discussions, problem solving and idea generation	• Quieter participants may not get the chance to share their great ideas – make sure everyone gets some space to talk
PowerPoint presentation	• Provides the presenter with prompts, and captures key content in writing	• The audience may stop listening and just read the slides instead

Evaluation

The intended outcome of the triple 'communicate' plan is that employees hear, understand and connect to your messages. At each of the three stages, it is therefore valuable to measure the effectiveness of that stage, and to be aware of what messages have landed and with what interpretations. This will help you to consider your reiterations and your final conformations, tailoring them to ensure that they fill any gaps left or correct any misdirections from the previous stages. The simplest way to do this is just to ask people:

- What have they understood from the communication?
- Do they understand the relevance of the messages for them?
- What else would they like to know?
- How did they feel about the medium used to communicate it (ie e-mail, face to face, etc)?

Gathering this feedback informally will provide some indications of the effectiveness, and help you to shape future iterations and future communications more generally. Ideally, at each stage in the triple communicate plan, you will see a deeper understanding or interpretation of the messaging.

You may find that feedback reports the communication as repetitive. Don't allow that to deter you from your three-stage plan. Remember that it is much better to be accused of overcommunicating rather than not communicating enough. You may just want to consider a greater variety of media, of presenter, of format, and a different way to promote the same key messages.

15   The stand-up

The stand-up is a short, sharp approach to meetings at work. Usually the stand-up happens in an open-plan area, or in someone's office space, with all participants standing for the duration of the meeting. This approach encourages people to engage, to stay on track, to keep contributions relevant and punchy, and to discuss rather than present. Typically it should be no more than 15 minutes in duration, and is used for project or team updates on a regular basis. Usually the purpose is informative, rather than to solve problems or generate ideas.

Research has suggested that the attention span of humans could be as lows as eight seconds, so to get the best out of people it is important to do all that we can to keep focus in meetings and discussions (Watson, 2015). Keeping it short, ensuring it is relevant and useful, and encouraging participation will all encourage team members to engage more fully in the process.

Best when

The stand-up is most effective when used as a regular team or operational meeting that can be effective with a narrow focus. It does not provide opportunity for long discussion, or for building relationships, but can work well if you want to provide short verbal updates, make quick decisions or redirect efforts. The focus will be short-term actions rather than long-term planning.

Best for

The stand-up is not a hierarchical approach – it brings the relevant people into a room, regardless of seniority, function or role. The meeting will need to be controlled by one person (the chair or facilitator) but this does not have to be the manager – it has to be someone who can effectively manage the process.

Resources

The stand-up does not require any resources. It can take place in an open-plan space so you don't even need a meeting room; it takes a short amount of time; and no AV equipment is needed.

Outcomes

The aim of this approach is to focus a team on short-term actions and focused plans or problems. The outcome should be a clear alignment with all the relevant parties in the room at the same time.

Process

1 Establish the guidelines for the stand-up approach. People will need to know and understand what is expected of them in the session (ie how to present, no long discussions, decision-focused, short term, no AVs, etc).

2 Define the purpose of the sessions – the stand-up approach may have a limited life span, for example for a specific project or initiative, or it may form part of your regular governance meetings. Be clear about the objective, and check regularly to ensure that you are meeting that objective.

3 Run the meetings. Keep a check on time and control the degree of debate. Keep your mind focused on the objectives or agenda, and challenge if the discussion goes off course. Where necessary, arrange for follow-up discussions outside of the meeting.

4 Evaluate the effectiveness of the stand-up in the context of your meeting purpose – and adapt it if necessary.

Hints and tips

- When to do a stand-up will depend on the purpose and frequency. Friday is good to review what you did in the previous few days, but not a great day to plan ahead. Monday is good to set the week's goals or outline focus areas, to establish a 'fresh start'. Wednesday can be effective to make sure you are on track and set corrective actions if you are not.

- As the name suggests, keep people standing up wherever possible. Once participants sit down and get comfortable, they may be more inclined to enter into longer discussion, or get distracted.

- Consider a 'no-phones' guideline – if the session is only 15 minutes, you can ask for participants' total focus during that time. The smartphone is the greatest distraction – research suggests that we check our phones up to 85 times a day (Woollaston, 2015)! Encourage people to leave it behind for just 15 minutes and see if it makes a difference to the team's focus.

- Stick to the principle that there should be no presentations, no PowerPoints, no pre-read and no minutes. Whilst those media and mechanisms are important in more formal meetings, they serve to distract in the stand-up.

- A sample mandate for the stand-up is shown in Table 2.3. Consider using a similar template to provide structure to your other meetings, and look for clear purpose, overlap of functionality in meetings (meetings that cover the same things) and overload in particular roles (the same people attending all the meetings).

Table 2.3 Sample meeting mandate for a stand-up

	MANDATE: Stand-Up Meeting	
	What to Include	**A Stand-Up Example**
Focus	Describe the key topics and the time horizon of your discussions.	• Project X – progress review
Frequency/ Duration	When will the meeting happen and how long for?	• Weekly • 15 minutes
Purpose	Why are you meeting?	• To check progress of the project • To allocate any outstanding actions • To address any roadblocks
Objectives	What objectives do you have for the stand-up?	• Ensure the project team is up to date • Ensure roadblocks are addressed • Follow up outstanding actions • Ensure stakeholders are being effectively managed
Input	What inputs are there to the discussion? Participants may need to be aware of these, pre-read them, and/or bring them to the meeting.	• Project objectives/brief • Project milestone plan • Risks and issues register
Process	A typical agenda – what will you discuss and how?	• Review actions this week – reallocate outstanding actions • Review risks and issues – allocate actions • Review what will happen next week – allocate ownership
Output	What do you expect to come out of the meeting – decisions, measures, reports, actions etc?	• Decisions and actions to progress project
Attendees	Who should attend (job titles rather than individual names) – and what is the role they play?	• Project sponsor • Project manager (chair) • Project team members • Project workstream leads

Evaluation

There are two levels to consider when evaluating the stand-up. The first is focused on the process, and takes into account the mechanisms of the process. Take stock of whether you are sticking to the time restrictions – how long are your sessions actually taking? Are the right people attending? Are your discussions focused? Are you avoiding PowerPoints and minutes?

At the next level of evaluation, you should consider the effectiveness of the approach. Consider whether the meetings are keeping people informed, or are they repeating what people already know? Are you driving actions and focusing on short-term goals? Is the stand-up helping to keep you on track, or making no difference to your progress? How many corrective actions are arising from your stand-up that could make the difference between success and failure? Who is contributing in the discussions?

These kinds of questions will help you to determine whether the stand-up is appropriate and/or making a difference to your team and its goals.

16   Media training

A training session or workshop on the techniques of media training – which might include self-presentation, message clarity and personal impact – can encourage your leaders or project teams to develop and align key messages for a change/vision and present them effectively.

The experience of media training should not be reserved for the very few people in your organization who may have cause to participate in television, radio or newspaper interviews. As a training event it provides a great opportunity for leaders to consider how they present themselves, and the clarity and alignment of the key messages delivered by a leadership group to the wider organization, as well as potentially to external audiences.

The Huffington Post (Pollard, 2015) identified 'five reasons why you need media training':

1 Learn how to speak in a way that people take notice.

2 Clearly and concisely define your key messages.

3 Develop prepared responses to difficult questions.

4 Learn to control the interview.

5 You are less likely to get misquoted.

These are all highly relevant to leaders delivering important communications internally within the workplace, and the principles of media training can therefore be extremely beneficial in preparing, aligning and delivering your messages to your employee groups. Ensuring that how you communicate as a leader is effective will be one of the core skills to build as your career develops. It supports the engagement of your leadership or project team by bringing the group together to agree and commit to an aligned set of messages on a specific subject or initiative.

Best when

Media training is beneficial when you have important messages to get across to the people in your business. When significant decisions are made, particularly those that may impact the future of your workforce, getting the communication right will be a key success factor, and this training will support that need.

However, this is also very relevant when you want to launch your strategy, or begin your objectives cascade process (consider the chapter 'Making connections' in Section 14 of this book). A leadership team that is fully aligned behind common messaging and key soundbites will communicate most effectively when together, but importantly when back in their own functional groups, and externally.

Best for

Media training will be advantageous for the senior management group who lead the business, a specific initiative, or who lead and sponsor a significant business decision.

It is important to consider the seniority of the group as the selection of people who will lead and deliver the message. It is also important to bring them into this learning as one cohesive group – there will be benefits of them working collaboratively to agree and define key messages as one team. It ensures that they are all 'bought in' to what will be communicated.

Resources

You will need to invest in media training. To make it effective, find an experienced media trainer – preferably one who has worked as a journalist, presenter or editor. This will not come cheap – apart from the actual cost of an experienced trainer it is likely that the costs will also need to cover AV equipment, telephony simulations and a camera person with their kit.

Outcomes

Media training will encourage the development of aligned messaging soundbites and key phrases to ensure that as a leadership team you communicate the same story, with the same emphasis. It provides the opportunity to develop your 'one single version of the truth'.

It will help your team to gain shared understanding on specific issues and on the approach you will take, and increase understanding/buy-in both internally and externally. It will help individuals to increase insight into their communication style and its impact on target audiences, as well as maximize the effectiveness of communication style.

Process

1 Identify, or seek out, a reputable media skills trainer. Ask for recommendations from others who have done similar activities before.

2 Brief them about your specific requirement. Be clear about whether your participants will be working with the media or whether you are looking to use the session for your internal communications practices only.

3 Run the programme for a leadership team, ensuring discretion and confidentiality for the learning process (media training can be fun, but some find it very difficult).

4 At the end of the session, capture your key learnings and your key messages – and ensure these form a key part of your stakeholder and communication strategy.

Hints and tips

It can be very effective to run your media training based around your specific challenge. For example, if you are ready to launch and cascade your new vision and strategy, or if you are about to announce a major restructure, providing that information to your trainer as the basis of your session will mean that you can work on real materials through the training, and come out with some clear communications messages.

Evaluation

Evaluate the effectiveness of the trainer using a standard happy-sheet evaluation (an example is provided in Table 16.2 at the end of this book).

At a deeper level, consider evaluation of the team's ability to implement the lessons learnt and deliver common messaging. What level of alignment do you have? Do you feel more confident to respond to questions and challenges, as well as more effective in your presentation delivery?

Further than that, consider the effectiveness of your overall communication as you proceed through the initiative.

17 Artistry

Artistry aims to bring out the creative side in your team members. In this activity, your team members are asked to draw a picture that represents the vision for the business, the team goal, or whatever you decide within the brief. It allows participants to be unconstrained by the use of words, and you can often tell a great deal about how your team members are interpreting the vision by the pictures that they draw.

Best when

This activity works well when you are looking to launch or engage your employees in a new or updated vision statement or set of goals. It works with large or small teams and can be a fun ice-breaker at the start of a workshop, or a good summary or review at the end.

Best for

This works with most employee groups but you may find that some don't see this as a credible activity. Introducing it as a bit of fun can minimize that risk. Even if the activity is not embraced, go with it, persevere. Encourage everyone to have a go, and see what results they produce. However, do think before you embark on this idea about how it will be perceived by your participants.

Resources

To be effective you need to encourage some creativity, and to do that you need to provide a range of materials. Provide flipchart paper if you can or a large-sized (A5+) artist pad. plus a selection of pens and pencils with different textures, thicknesses and colours. If you want to take it a step further, bring other craft materials (ribbons, glitter, glue, magazines etc). You will need space for people to spread out and get creative.

Outcomes

Hopefully participants will enjoy this activity and have some fun with it. But in addition to having fun, they should be able to demonstrate a connection to the goals or vision. They will have drawn something that shows their interpretation, and this personal connection to a vision is more likely to make them feel engaged with it.

Process

1 Provide each participant with art materials at their creative station – their own set of paper and pens.

2 Describe the brief – they are to create a picture that represents how they see the vision/goal etc. Give them a time limit and let them get creative. Encourage them to wander around for inspiration if they are struggling to get into a creative mindset.

3 Once all the pictures are complete, ask each participant to describe what they have drawn and why. This helps to understand their perception of and connection to the strategy. Point out where interesting, contradictory or complementary messages are heard among participants.

Hints and tips

- Encourage the use of pictures only, not words, in the artwork. However, some people might really find it difficult to draw, so after some encouragement you may want to relax your stance on that. It can be just as interesting to see what words are picked out. Forcing people to draw can be disengaging – and that is not part of the goal!

- If a participant is finding it difficult to get started you can take time to remind them of the vision or goal they are drawing about and ask them – what does it mean for you? How do you interpret that? How might it look? Close your eyes, what do you imagine when you think of that?

- Ask an independent party (maybe a facilitator or meeting host) to be the judge and award prizes (give out rosettes if your budget can stretch to them). Choose categories such as 'best use of colour', 'most abstract' or 'top artist'.

- After the workshop, arrange to have the pictures displayed in the style of an art gallery around the office. This will promote discussion about the vision and help both to translate it on 'the floor' and keep it alive.

Evaluation

Of course, you are not looking to evaluate artistic prowess here – this is about what has been attempted to be drawn, rather than the quality of the artwork! So give some consideration to the following questions:

- What have participants depicted in their artwork? Are you noticing strong personal perspectives on the vision, or more generic interpretations?
- Are all the pictures aligned to the vision – are there any to suggest that the participant has not fully understood or correctly interpreted what it is that you are trying to achieve? If so, you may want to follow up after the session.

18 Dream clouds

The 'dream cloud' activity invites participants to consider and articulate their future vision. Dependent on the question you ask, it might be in the context of the team, its performance, the wider organization or a vision of where we all want to be. Participants are asked to finish the sentence 'I have a dream...' using their own words.

Best when

This activity can work particularly well at the opening or closing of a workshop, especially when focused around objective setting or thinking about future vision or goals. It can also be used as an effective 'ice-breaker' or warm-up to an event or meeting.

Best for

This is a simple activity where everyone can join in. It is most effective if participation is encouraged at all levels of seniority and in all functions and job types. This typically works best with smaller groups (up to around 12 people) but can also be done in significantly larger groups if sharing and discussion is minimized.

Resources

Ideally you will need some card in the shape of a cloud or speech bubbles – some different aesthetics can be inspiring. However, a Post-it note, plain card or a flipchart will do just fine. You can always encourage people to cut out their own dream-cloud shape! Bring some coloured marker pens and, if you can, bring a camera to take photographs of the clouds.

Outcomes

Each person has verbalized their goal or dream related to the workshop you have run. By sharing it with the rest of the team the aspiration becomes well known and this could be beneficial in making it a reality.

In addition, team members get to see and hear each other's goals. They can begin to make connections and see where they have similar or contradictory goals, how they can help each other or where they may get in each other's way, and some discussion about the collective achievement of all the goals can give team members a real boost about all that they can achieve.

Process

1 Decide when the dream clouds will be useful in your process. At the start of a workshop it can help you to gauge how much alignment you have in the views of the team and the individual perspectives of each. At the end of a session you may find it a useful evaluation tool.

2 Hand out the cards and pens. Ask participants to complete the sentence or phrase 'I have a dream...'

3 Allow participants to take a few minutes of quiet contemplation. This should be an individual exercise not a group discussion, but it is important to recognize that some may prefer to discuss with others in order to get inspiration.

4 In turn, ask each participant to describe their dream or goal and why it is important to them or to the business. Invite comments or questions from the rest of the group for clarification, or to explore any opportunities to work together, etc.

5 Explain what will happen next to the dream clouds, and what you as manager will do to help people to achieve their goal or work towards that dream.

Hints and tips

- If you run this exercise with a large group, rather than initiating group discussion ask people to wander around the room clearly displaying their dream cloud to others. Encourage them to stop each other to ask questions one to one, or to find people in the room who have a similar, contradictory or supporting dream and discuss what this might mean. This encourages collaboration, but in a larger group where collective discussion is less practical it engages the people who will most benefit from connecting with each other.

- Ask each person to write their name on the back of the cloud so that you can keep track of whose is whose.

- Take fun photographs of people with their dream cloud – not just a portrait but something entertaining and eye-catching. Pictures with groups together all holding their clouds can also work well.

- Use a wall space back in the office to display the clouds – this shows a collective view of the dreams of your team.
- Ask people to display their cloud on their desk. A bit like the commitment card described in Section 1 of this book, visibility will serve as a reminder and/or a motivator, as well as a talking point among colleagues and visitors.

Evaluation

Ask participants to bring their cloud with them to future meetings and talk about progress, and whether the dream cloud has had any influence on how they work (individually or collectively). Find out if they would now want to change the dream, and what might have influenced that decision.

Discuss with participants whether they consider that the organization, the team or themselves individually are actively working towards the dream, or whether they want to or should be doing so. If so, work with them to develop a plan to advocate and/or take action.

Engaging the organization   03

19 Top team representative

A consultative committee or employee representative communication group can serve a great purpose – or can purely meet the legal obligations required by organizations. Having an employee representative participate in your leadership team takes employee involvement to another level.

Best when

This initiative is most effective when your leadership team is mature, has worked together for some time and is effective. It will be counterproductive to have an employee representative present to experience the 'storming' phases of your team relationship or to be caught up in the crossfire of issues that have not yet been resolved within the team.

It is best when you have a regular heartbeat of management meetings with a clear agenda and governance structure. This means that the employee representative can be clear about what to expect.

Best for

An employee representative from 'the floor' should be able to represent all functions and all levels of the organization in leadership team meetings. It is not important to consider their function, seniority or tenure with the company. What is important is that they have a proactive interest in taking on the role, and they have support from and are seen as a credible representative by their colleagues.

Resources

You might consider the time for training or briefing your representative and the time it might take to give feedback to or collate considerations of the employee group.

The employee representative may require access to technology (e-mail, a laptop) that they do not have already to facilitate their work as a rep. You will need to provide this equipment to enable them to fulfil the role.

Outcomes

Having a representative on your leadership team can begin to break down barriers between leadership and management, and will be seen as an advantageous step in the involvement of employees in business decision making.

Process

1 Communicate the intent to establish the representative on your leadership team. Include information about the remit the rep will have, the scope, confidentiality, etc. Importantly, explain the rationale – why you are launching this initiative.

2 Confirm the election process – see the guidance below in 'Hints and tips'.

3 Provide a written briefing to those interested in standing for election that includes a 'job description' outlining responsibilities, and information about the commitment required and the tenure.

4 Invite nominations, and run the election process. You may need to allow some time for nominees to canvas for votes and promote their own proposition.

5 Communicate to the organization to confirm the successfully elected representative, and the next steps.

6 Brief the representative about their role, and what happens next. It may be important to confirm the confidentiality requirements, asking the representative to sign a confidentiality agreement if that is appropriate.

7 Provide a meeting schedule to the representative. At the first meeting, make introductions as necessary and confirm each person's role at the meeting. Introduce the rep to any meeting 'etiquette' you may have established (eg mobile phone use, agendas and minutes, etc).

8 During the meeting, engage the representative in the discussions and encourage their contribution. Recognize that there may be some discussions that have to happen without the representative present, and be transparent about that.

9 Agree what can be shared outside of the meeting, and what must remain confidential. Encourage cascade of information wherever appropriate.

Hints and tips

- There will need to be recognition on both sides that there will always be some issues that are sufficiently sensitive that the employee representative may need to be excused – especially commercially sensitive topics, sensitive or confidential employee issues or decisions that might impact ways of working.

- Consider recognition reward for a job well done, but also be ready to address performance issues if the representative does not meet expectations in fulfilling the role.

- Use the representative. Don't just have them as a token gesture – encourage them to research issues, to bring feedback from the floor and ensure they contribute a different perspective to the discussions.

The election process

Personnel Today (July 2011) provided the following short guidelines on how to run a fair election process:

- Votes can be cast secretly, and must be counted accurately.

- All employees are given the right to vote.

- No affected employee is unreasonably refused from standing for election.

- A sufficient number of representatives is determined to ensure that the interests of all the affected employees will be represented.

The most important thing for you to remember is that the election process must be fair. You should ensure that the process is as well-managed as possible, from preparing for the election to announcing the results. You should consider the following questions:

- What type of election process will be used? Postal, via e-mail or held in the workplace?

- Will the voters be divided into constituencies, according to geography or seniority, or will the entire workforce be treated as a single electorate?

- How many representatives will be elected?

- How long will the representatives' term of office last?

- How long will the entire process take? Employees must be invited to elect representatives in sufficient time to begin consultation.

Evaluation

Check the representative's level of engagement:

- Are they just attending or are they really participating?
- Is appropriate information flowing from the floor to the team and vice versa?
- Are they proactively seeking opinion from those they represent?
- Are they proactively raising issues, and tabling them at the appropriate meetings?
- Are they fairly representing the leadership team process, discussions and decisions?

Ensure that feedback is provided to the representative related to the evaluation, and provide them with the support and opportunity they need to perform the role to their best.

In employee opinion surveys or pulse checks, find out what employees are saying about the representative and their role on the team. Do employees feel they have more access to senior leaders or to their discussions and decisions? Is their contribution valued by those they represent?

20 Top team unplugged

The top team unplugged event is an opportunity for employees to attend an open forum with senior leaders within the organization. Unplugged is distinct from other top team communications sessions because it typically has no formal structure and it keeps the floor open for all employees to ask questions on any topic. There are no visuals, no slides or scripts. The most technology required could be a microphone – if the room size or audience size require it. It is an open dialogue session with your top team and a group of employees.

Best when

This will work well as an effective engagement tool if you have a strong and competent leadership team who are comfortable, accustomed and accomplished at public speaking. The ability to work without detailed scripting, without slides and without a known agenda is a critical success factor. Leaders who have successfully been through media training or have experience at public speaking will be well suited.

It is a particularly useful activity when your business is going through change. Employees like to feel that they have direct access to sources of information (leaders) and that they have the opportunity to provide feedback and challenge.

Best for

You could approach this in one of two ways. In a large company it could be a great way to keep your management population engaged, spreading key messages and developing advocacy and alignment. In smaller organizations, bringing all employees together will work effectively.

Resources

The top team unplugged is extremely resource light. Other than the time for the event and maybe a microphone there is nothing you need. It is an activity that can be done anywhere – a meeting room, a canteen, the open-plan office – at any time.

Outcomes

Unplugged encourages visibility and accessibility of senior managers, allowing dialogue, questions, debate and feedback. It aims to strengthen communication channels and the flow of information, building trust and maintaining open communication lines.

Process

1 Prepare your leaders first. Make sure that they are well trained and briefed, and able to openly and honestly respond to challenges from the floor (media training, as outlined in Section 2 of this book, is a great preparation for this type of activity).

2 Keep the environment relaxed. Arrange for chairs or stools for the top team. Avoid desks and tables that make it more formal and can create a barrier. Organize enough chairs for the audience rather than standing, arranged informally rather than in fixed rows in order to encourage discussion. If you are able to provide refreshments, then this is an added bonus.

3 Invite your attendees, confirming the purpose or key discussion points of the session, and any guidance that you want to set. You might encourage people to think about some questions before they come along, for example, or to mix up teams rather than everyone sitting with their usual colleagues.

4 It is best if you can leave the agenda open and not ask for questions up front – but if you have to, make that clear in advance.

5 Ensure that the panel encourages discussion/dialogue through their own part of the session. For example, encouragement to have a short discussion about a topic with colleagues sat close by might prompt smaller groups to ask questions or offer comment.

6 Close the session by thanking the audience for attending, your top team for participating, and explain what will happen next – ie are there any unanswered questions or actions to follow up on? Will you hold another session? Do you want the attendees to share the information they have heard in the unplugged session? Make sure that any actions are allocated before your team leaves.

Hints and tips

- Be really clear about your intentions. If you intend to do this quarterly or monthly, for example, ensure that you deliver on that commitment. If it is an ad hoc event then be clear about that too. Managing expectations will reduce the risks of the process – and you – losing credibility.

- If you position it as informal, make it informal. Dress appropriately, don't sit behind a desk to talk, don't use any slides and don't read from a script.

Evaluation

The usual happy-sheet evaluation will help you to gauge whether people enjoyed the event, and whether it met the objectives you set (an example is provided at the back of this book). You could also consider using the mood board (see Section 2) and/or the graffiti wall (see later in Section 3).

Given the criticality of the boss's performance, this is an important part of the evaluation. How was their delivery? How engaging were they? What key messages have people taken away with them? And are those key messages the ones you had hoped people would take away?

21 The marketplace

The internal marketplace brings together all of your main functions in one place to promote their function, share information about what they do and build better relationships between teams. The process asks for each function to provide an informal display or static presentation – like you might find at a trade show or business fair – and allows all employees the opportunity to walk around, engage with the different teams and learn something new about the business or their colleagues.

> 'You can make more friends in two months by becoming interested in other people than you can in two years by trying to get other people interested in you.'
>
> *Dale Carnegie*

Best when

This activity works well when you want to improve the understanding of the different departments in your business. You can use this experience to build team work and collaboration and to identify opportunities to improve the effectiveness of teams.

Best for

The internal marketplace works best when everyone can get involved. Engaging your whole team to build a stand or presentation, and empowering all team members to participate in manning your stand will keep them involved, and give them a stimulus to connect with others on the day. Don't leave it to your senior managers to represent the function.

Resources

To be impactful you will need to invest in this process. You should consider the value of really theming the event as a marketplace – organize real market stalls and prepare the presentation and display materials as professionally as you can. However, this should not be a barrier. If the best you can manage is a flipchart with some key bullet points about the team, then it will still serve the purpose.

You will need to invest time. This is most effective when everyone downs tools and attends at the same time, so if you are able to, shut down your operation for a couple of hours in order to get the best possible interaction and engagement. Alternatively you can run the marketplace over an extended lunch period, allowing employees the opportunity to explore during their break. Bear in mind, though, that this is likely to be a more voluntary approach. Investing the time out of your business – if practical – will be beneficial.

Outcomes

The primary aim of the internal marketplace is to enable your teams and functions to get to know each other better in order to understand more about what they do. You can develop this outcome to the next level by using the event as an opportunity to identify opportunities to collaborate more effectively, to understand what needs to happen in the hand-off process from one to another to make it most effective and to understand individual roles in the process.

Process

1 Before your commit to running a marketplace event, take some time to really consider why it is important for you and your business at this time, and what you want to achieve through the event.

2 Engage with functional leads to encourage them to advocate the event and lead from the front in preparing for and committing to the marketplace.

3 Communicate news of the event and its objectives. Explain what you are planning to do, and why, with a clear indication of why employees will benefit by attending.

4 Brief the display teams. Those employees who have been nominated or have agreed to prepare and be the 'crew' for the display for their teams should be briefed on any design issues, key messaging and what types of things they might display. Ideally they should have some freedom to create their own content, but there may be some elements that you would prefer were common among all displayers (for example, some headings on what the department does, or an organization chart).

5 On the day, identify a few employees to run the set-up of the event, ensuring that the participants know where they need to be, what they need to do, and to support any ongoing needs that they have during the day.

6 Run the session. Encourage employees to attend by providing prompts on the day. Your leaders and managers should be strong advocates of the event and should allow people time to attend, and of course should be seen to attend themselves.

7 Send out your thanks. You should thank the display participants for taking the time to prepare and make the event happen, and you should thank your teams for taking some time out to talk to the participants. A reminder to both sets of parties on what was achieved by doing so, and maybe some highlights of the day, will also be beneficial.

8 Evaluate the effectiveness of the session, using some of the suggestions later in this section. Bear in mind that you should evaluate not just the immediate effectiveness of the event (ie did people enjoy attending?) but the longer-term impacts that relate to collaboration and teamwork.

Hints and tips

Encourage participants to make their way to every stall or presentation by offering incentive. If each employee had a 'passport' that they had to get stamped at each stand, there could be a small reward at the end of their journey – a chocolate bar or a coffee, for example.

Alternatively, organize a quiz – preferably one in which participants who have visited all of the stands are more likely to perform well.

Evaluation

The 'happy sheet' style of evaluation will capture some immediate reactions (an example is provided in Table 16.2 at the end of this book) – whether people enjoyed the event, found it useful, liked the environment, etc – so as an initial level of evaluation this can be valuable.

However, some of the less obvious evaluation questions can probably be asked some time after the event has taken place. For example: are you seeing a greater level of understanding between departments? And, if so, what are you seeing or hearing that leads you to that? Have the interactions between the teams led to improvements or efficiencies in process?

22 Common cause

Encouraging your team to support a common goal is a well-known approach for engaging employees. Sometimes taking it beyond the sphere of work targets and goals can be helpful in building relationships, breaking down silos and learning some valuable lessons about working together effectively.

Bringing people together to support a charitable cause can do just that whilst at the same creating benefits for the charities involved. Although this may seem like a distraction to the day job it is important to keep sight of the benefits it can bring – and to recognize that there will most likely be a commitment to activities, planning and involvement outside of working hours too.

Research has shown that employees connect emotionally to the company when they are involved in donating and volunteering for charity, and a report by the organization Network for Good on their website (www.networkfor-good.com) states: 'Employee engagement through cause is a vital means by which to strengthen employee relationships, enhance employee morale and even build critical skill sets and expertise. Plus, employees are hungry for ways to get involved in a cause.'

Best when

There is no bad time to focus on good causes and generating charitable donations. However, it is always worth considering what else is happening in your organization at the time. If you are experiencing difficult financial circumstances, or employees feel concerned about their stability or security of employment, it may not be the best time to kick off this initiative.

Best for

The common cause will engage all of your employees but works most effectively when a range of functions, departments and levels of seniority are involved. It provides an opportunity for those with interest, rather than status, to lead an initiative or activity, and this should be encouraged wherever possible. Providing this opportunity for personal development may add some value to some of the participants.

Resources

You will need to consider whether you want to allocate resources, time and funds to the common-cause initiative. You could entirely limit it to activities in free time and no matched funding, but this could seem at odds with having the common-cause initiative in the first place.

Allocating a budget, however small, will demonstrate your commitment but may also develop some financial awareness capabilities within the common-cause teams.

Don't forget that sponsorship is often an opportunity for company promotion too. Your company logo on a fun runners' kit, for example, might bring you exposure to new clients – and any opportunity to feature the common-cause initiatives in local, international or social media will provide great free publicity and promote your company's social responsibility. You should therefore consider some financial contribution as an investment – and consider its returns.

Outcomes

The primary and worthy beneficiaries of a common-cause initiative are the charities that take donations and raise their own profiles through your organization – and aiming to satisfy some of their needs (be it funds, time or profile) is one of the key outcomes of this initiative.

However, in the process you are likely see some benefits for your employees and your organization too. You may see demonstrations of talents that you would not see through an employee's day-to-day work, such as event-planning skills, leadership capability, financial management, and team management or co-ordination. As employees are given the opportunity to demonstrate other skills, they should also be recognized and, wherever possible, utilized.

Process

1 Establish a charity committee. Encourage attendance from across all levels of seniority, all functions or departments and, if appropriate and practical, all locations.

2 Set, or develop with the committee, the terms of reference, detailing what you want them to do, and how to do it. This might include the charity selection, the type of events, and any guidelines about use of company time and other resources.

3 Agree a review process that will ensure that the committee continues to be effective, both in raising money and profile for chosen charities, and for engaging employees.

Hints and tips

- Consider how you will select the charities who will benefit from this initiative. Asking for suggestions from your employees, and varying the chosen charities, might seem more engaging, but there is some suggestion that a top-down approach (ie the organization selecting its charity of the year and sticking to fundraising for one cause) can be more engaging for employees.

- Agree some principles in advance. For example, will you match donations or top up? Will you allow any time off? Can you support activities in the working environment - eg can people bring in cakes, is it okay to have fancy dress? The more open you can be the better, but where you do have clear operational reasons for being more restrictive be clear about the rationale. Don't just say no.

- Join in!

Evaluation

Focus your evaluation on the charitable nature of the common-cause initiative. How much money has been raised, how many activities have taken place and what has been the participation rate among your employees?

The committee should consider whether it has achieved its goals for the period under review. A lessons-learnt review could help to identify new approaches in order to get more involvement and to increase the funds raised.

By way of indirect evaluation, you might also consider whether your business is experiencing an increase in collaboration and communication across teams or departments as employees start to get involved.

23   Inspiring cinema club

Many organizations find great value in bringing guest speakers to their conferences or events, offering inspiring wisdom from the worlds of business, politics, sport or entertainment. But these can come at great cost, often out of reach of many larger businesses, never mind the smaller ones. However, the internet has provided a new opportunity with sites such as YouTube and TED Talks (others are available – see 'Hints and tips' below) providing the streaming of similar talks for free. The cinema club uses these opportunities to play out inspirational 'guest speakers' and makes such inspirational talks much more accessible for your employees.

It is engaging because employees want to be inspired, and whilst your own leaders might do that well it is interesting to hear specialist and/or external ideas and perspectives.

Best when

This is a great idea at any time. You may want to theme your 'showings' to issues or opportunities you are facing in your business, or connect them to an ongoing programme of development.

Best for

This is an effective approach for all employees. This will work well if it is open rather than limited to certain groups or levels. Open invitations will suggest who is interested in a subject and/or keen to develop and be inspired.

Resources

You will need AV resources that are adequate for your audience and a suitable venue.

You might want to allow employees to attend in work time, in which case you need to factor this into your resource requirements. As recognition for their willingness to attend, consider providing the drinks and popcorn! Plan a budget that will allow you to make it a fun experience for those who choose to attend.

Outcomes

The cinema club is intended to be an opportunity for employees to mix with each other, to learn or be inspired from the talk that is viewed, and to explore some of those learnings with others who have experienced it with them. Of course, the viewings proposed here are all available to any individual at any time, so the real value is in presenting it in the workplace, perhaps with an internal facilitator to add to the process, and with other colleagues also present. It provides the opportunity to make new connections and to discuss how best to utilize new information from the showing.

Process

1 Appoint someone as the cinema club co-ordinator, and invite them to investigate and propose a cinema programme for a period of time (eg across a six-month period, with one showing per month).

2 Identify your venue and its optimum capacity. Ensure that it has appropriate equipment for showing the selected videos on a big screen from the internet – ie it should have good Wi-Fi connections, internet access (no IT-policy blocking sites), connection to a PC or laptop and a large screen clearly visible to all seated attendees. It is better not to have a table in the room, and to make the seating arrangement as informal as possible.

3 Fix the schedule for your cinema club – how often it will play out; what themes you want to include, when. Once you have the detail, provide information on specific showings and availability.

4 Communicate the rationale (why you are launching it), the objectives of the initiative (what you hope to get out of it, as well as what attendees can hope to gain) and the process for booking a seat.

5 Run the programme and monitor feedback continually, with a view to making improvements to the programme selection, the event set-up, etc.

6 If you choose to have a facilitator to run a discussion after the session, ensure they are familiar with the chosen programme and the key points that you might want to draw from it in the follow-up. Encourage the facilitator to prepare some open questions related to the programme in order to get the discussion flowing.

7 Reshape the approach if necessary and continue to run it.

Hints and tips

- As recognition for employees' willingness to attend, consider providing the drinks and popcorn!

- Try this initiative as a pilot, but don't limit the pilot to just one showing. You might find different levels of interest in different topic areas, so

showing a range of subjects at different times of the day will help you to
gauge the real levels of interest.

- Ask the audience. In your initial communication about the club, ask for
feedback about what people would like to see. You might want to offer
some prompting headings.

- Hold a discussion group afterwards. If your group is too big for that you
could try some dialogue sheets or dream clouds (see the relevant chapters
in Section 2).

- Consider the process for attending – do you want to issue tickets, have
an attendee list or keep it as first come first served? This may depend on
your seating capacity, but the more flexible it is, the more it may appeal
to some people.

- Useful websites include TED Talks; a useful series is *Undercover Boss*
(available on YouTube); film documentaries might also be available
via sites such as Netflix and Amazon, but do check the broadcasting
permissions.

- Check the permission related to broadcasting before you show any
videos or films. TED's website provides permission for you to broadcast quite freely – provided you follow certain conditions, but they do
allow for you to broadcast in the cinema-club style. Before you do, check
the terms on their website: https://www.ted.com/about/our-organization/
our-policies-terms/ted-talks-usage-policy

Evaluation

At a basic level, how is your attendance? Are people showing interest and is
their interest followed up through actual attendance?

At the next level, how engaged are attendees with the subject matter?
Happy sheets will give an indication but you might also hear informal feedback on the grapevine. Establishing discussion groups might also give an
opportunity to test how things have landed.

Harder to assess, but perhaps more meaningful, is to consider the impact
it has on engagement. Is the intent to inspire having a material effect on how
employees are working, their behaviours or their innovation?

24　The columnist

Take a look at your internal communications methods – whether it be team briefings, a newsletter or an intranet, these are typically developed by either communications specialists or functional experts in the subjects that are being written about. The columnist takes a different approach, and encourages volunteers from any function or level in your business to become an internal 'reporter' or 'journalist'. They can develop articles and features that are led from the 'bottom up', with issues or topics that are identified by employees, rather than being 'news' determined by those who want to tell it. It could be a one-off experience focusing on a specific issue, or it could be a longer-term responsibility, contributing on a regular basis.

The columnist empowers volunteers to identify, research and write on issues that matter to the 'floor'. This is likely to mean that senior managers are interviewed and can have a say, but editorially they will have to allow the content of that column to be driven by the author.

Best when

Ideally you will already have an internal communications intranet, newsletter or magazine – but don't let the absence of one stop you from considering this process. You could make this your starting point.

You may want to prepare your managers or leaders to be interviewed prior to launching this initiative. Briefing them on the relevant subject matter, key messages, etc – and ensuring that they understand any confidential areas – will help to ensure that the journalist's article remains relevant and aligned.

Best for

Encouraging a range of contributions from all levels and functions in the organization will allow your publication to be more representative of your employee group. By encouraging broader communications, and a relatively open approach to the topics covered, you will be reporting on issues that are of interest to your workforce.

Resources

Your columnist will need to spend company time on the article – identifying, researching and writing. You may want to put a guideline around how much time this is. They will also need access to a PC.

Outcomes

The primary outcome for the columnist initiative is to be able to communicate from a 'bottom-up' view of the organization. It will help to get engagement from employees with articles written that are meaningful for them, as materials are written from their perspective, potentially encouraging a wider readership.

Process

1 After communicating the vision/objectives, etc, invite volunteers to take on the role of 'journalist'.

2 Allow the journalists access to the senior team for one-on-one interviews about the vision, the company goals and maybe some company history. Allowing the journalist some freedom about the subject matter will add to their level of interest.

3 Allow the journalist team to put together a series of articles for the newspaper – for example, a reflection of the vision/challenges from their perspective.

4 If the journalist team is comfortable with having full editorial rights then they should be allowed it, but you may want to get agreement that you will review the final content before you start.

OR

5 Allow the same process on a regular basis by asking volunteers to take on the role of 'columnist' in your existing regular publications.

Hints and tips

- Use both a top-down and a bottom-up approach. Encourage volunteer reporters from senior levels in the organization to investigate or write articles that encourage them to go 'back to the floor' and talk to people on the front line. Encourage reporters from more junior levels to challenge senior managers in the delivery of their articles.

- Don't let it be all about the cleanliness of the toilets or the quality of the lunch facilities – but do recognize that these may be important issues for some.

Evaluation

Are you getting volunteers or asking people to do it? The less you have to encourage people to volunteer as journalists, the better. Volunteering shows an interest, but you will also have to ensure that they are allowed some freedom in their writing, and that you won't edit them out – otherwise you will not get future or repeat volunteers.

What are they writing about? What subjects are interesting them, and/or others in the organization? This might lead you to a good understanding of some of the issues or challenges being experienced by your workforce. If you spot some themes, try to get into the issue in more detail, and see if there is anything you can do to help resolve it. And then write about it!

How much editorial control is being exerted? Too much might mean that you are not really empowering people. What feedback are you getting on the newsletter? What do readers want more of, or less of?

25   Birthday breakfast

The birthday itself is not a key factor in the birthday breakfast (unless you choose to make it one – see 'Hints and tips' below) – but it is the 'excuse' you might need or want in order to bring together a group of employees from across your business.

It is engaging because it provides access to senior managers in an informal environment. It provides the opportunity for a two-way exchange of information, views and ideas, but it also connects people from across your business who might not otherwise have cause to meet or chat.

Best when

This is best when your organization is large enough to make a monthly breakfast meeting worthwhile. Smaller groups of birthday guests will be far less intimidating than one-to-one breakfasts, but if you have smaller numbers you could run them quarterly instead.

It is also important that your managers are able to run such a meeting – a bit like 'top team unplugged' (see earlier in this section of the book) this is an informal meeting without script, and the person in charge needs to be an effective communicator, able to deal with the awkward silences and/or the challenging topics that could be brought up by any of the birthday guests.

Best for

All employees celebrating a birthday in a given month. Seniority, function, job and age are all irrelevant factors – if their birthday falls in that month (or quarter) they are invited.

Resources

Typically this is a short discussion session, so setting aside an hour should be sufficient time. Given the title, you will need to supply a breakfast, but this can be simply done on a small budget.

Outcomes

As a stand-alone activity the birthday breakfast provides a once-a-year opportunity for employees to engage in an informal discussion with senior managers. However, its intention is broader than that as is it should aim to break down barriers and open lines of communication across all functions and through all levels of the organization.

Process

1 Get a list of employees with birthdays in each month. Make sure you add your new starters and take out your leavers as the year progresses.

2 Invite birthday guests to your breakfast. Explain in the invitation what will happen over breakfast, as well as the timing and location. For larger groups consider having another management team representative present as well. This helps to manage the group, but also allows someone else to be the stimulus for conversation at times.

3 Organize breakfast, and maybe a cake or a small token birthday gift for each participant. A small box of chocolates or a bottle of wine would be a nice touch.

4 Prepare. Find out about the attendees and prepare some topics that you might want to discuss if the conversation slows.

5 Run the breakfast. Typically such events would run for about 45–60 minutes depending on the size of your group, and how engaged they are in the discussions.

6 Check for immediate feedback at the end of the session – ask what people liked about the session and what might improve it.

7 Take any lessons learnt into your next session.

Hints and tips

- Don't do it too early in the morning as it might put off some people.
- Don't assume that the conversation will flow. Prepare for the session with some good open-prompt questions. Assume that you will have to drive the conversation. It is a bonus if you don't. Think about some high-level topics that might be of interest to those attending – a particularly challenging account, a new customer, quality issues, a change in process, etc.
- Before the event, find out a little about the people attending. Be sure you know who they are, how long they have been employed by the company, what job they do, their strengths and any recent achievement. You might want to know if it is a significant birthday for them. You may also want to find out a few things about their personal situation as this can help

with the ice-breaking conversation – any children, where they live, holiday plans, etc.

- You may find that attendance is low. Use team leaders and managers to encourage people to attend where possible. If people don't know what to expect they may be nervous, so pushing through the first few events may be challenging but will create stories that could encourage participation.

Evaluation

The initial evaluation is on whether people attend or not. Encouraging attendance is fine but forcing it is not very engaging, so if birthday guests are attending voluntarily this suggests some success in the process.

How engaged are people in the discussion? Are people raising topics with you, or is the agenda driven by you?

From a company perspective you may be interested to evaluate the issues that you are able to discuss. What issues are people bringing to the table? However, the employees' perspective may be different – they may be more concerned with whether they felt they had been heard, and how they felt during the session.

26   Back to the floor

The boss, manager or leadership team member spends a day working 'on the floor' – be it a factory floor, retail floor, call centre, etc, working in the role alongside other employees. With no 'special treatment' this allows the opportunity to experience the working day as it is experienced every day by front-line staff. It provides opportunities to experience the highs and lows of the role and to identify problems and opportunities for improvement, efficiency, etc. Above all, it gives unparalleled access to the employee voice. Being able to listen to direct feedback and commentary from employees in your organization as they go about their daily routine is a rare honour and an opportunity that should be embraced and optimized.

It is engaging because it provides employees with access to senior managers but in their own environment. Employees are more likely to feel able to talk to managers openly; they will be able to demonstrate how things work in their area, and it will show that you care and that you are interested, particularly so if you are able to fix issues or address concerns.

This initiative is not about watching from afar, or catching people out, or hiding your identity to encourage honest feedback. You should be working alongside employees, doing the tasks, running a full day as they do and learning from them in the process. You should also not be focusing your attention on how people perform but rather on how they are enabled to perform – their processes, equipment, systems, etc.

Best when

Back to the floor will be most effective if you are genuinely interested in how your business is running at ground level. Don't pay lip service to it – employees will see through it and will be less likely to engage in the process.

Best for

Back to the floor is a great way to get your senior managers to understand and appreciate the work that happens at ground level in your business. Focus this initiative on your senior team, taking the opportunity to engage with teams in departments across the organization and at all levels.

Resources

Just time – but bear in mind that if you make a commitment to problem solve you have to put resources behind it to ensure it happens. That could be a small budget or it could be a significant team. So if you are not able to make that commitment to resources then think carefully about your approach, rationale, intentions and, importantly, the messaging about all of these things.

Outcomes

There are two directions of outcomes for this initiative. From the bottom up, employees should feel heard, appreciated and valued. They should feel that you have taken an interest in them and the work they do, and that any issues raised will be considered. From the top down, managers can get an appreciation of how things work in practice in the business; can make connections with employees; and can empathize, listen and problem solve.

Process

1 In your leadership or management team, agree the goals and objectives of a back to the floor programme. Once this is established you can consider who should participate, and where they should get their working experience.

2 Communicate the initiative to your employees. Explain what you are doing, why, and what you hope to achieve from the process. Explain in the communications what you expect from employees during a back to the floor experience (eg you want things to operate as normal, no special treatment; you want to hear what is working well and what could be improved, etc).

3 At the end of the experience, provide a feedback briefing to those you have been interacting with – some immediate initial thoughts about what you have experienced, what you liked, some things that you have learnt, etc. Providing this immediate feedback demonstrates that you have got some value from the experience.

4 Follow up on any actions or ideas that were raised during your time on the floor. Involve some of those you worked with on the day. The idea is not to push ownership back to managers, as by being aware you can take overall responsibility to resolve matters – but you don't have to do that on your own.

5 Share the outcomes of your experience with the wider organization, so that they get to hear about the initiative, how you benefitted from doing

it, and any changes that may have happened as a result (focusing on actions completed rather than promises).

Hints and tips

- Share insights from your experiences. Consider using a columnist (see earlier in this section) to help communicate it.

- Take action on issues that are raised – or provide feedback about why you cannot or will not.

- Schedule ahead. Get each of your management team to participate, visiting different parts of the floor across a year – or they could do them all.

- As much as you communicate what the process aims to achieve you might also find it useful to tell people what it is not, ie it is not a test or an evaluation; it is not an attempt to find out who is not busy; it is not a cost-saving exercise.

Evaluation

The evaluation for back to the floor should be focused on the 'so what?' of the experience from your perspective. For example, consider:

- What did you learn from the experience – about your business, your employees, processes, suppliers, customers, etc?

- What opportunities for improvement or efficiency have you uncovered?

- How many problems have you uncovered and fixed?

- What talent have you spotted, and what are you going to do with it?

- How much more accessible or approachable do you think you are as a result of having connected with people in this way?

27 Graffiti wall

The graffiti wall is a large-scale poster, often covering the large part of a hallway wall where there is high footfall, on which employees can note in brief their views and opinions. It is most effective when focused on a specific question rather than as a blank canvas, as employees then have some guidance about what areas to comment on. Sometimes the blank wall can be too intimidating!

The graffiti wall allows employees an opportunity to write or draw to express their thoughts on a given topic. CIPD research suggests that where organizations ask for contributions and opinions it is recognized that they genuinely want that input. This opportunity to listen to the 'employee voice' is seen as a foundation of employee engagement.

The graffiti wall provides one medium to listen to that voice. Ideally it should not be used in isolation, but as one approach in a suite of methodologies that enable an effective two-way dialogue between the organization and its employees. However, it is an engaging way of involving employees, allowing them maximum freedom of speech and expressing things in ways that are meaningful for them.

The critical success factor, however, is in using that feedback effectively. If employees feel heard, they are more likely to contribute to and engage in future dialogue.

Best when

The graffiti wall is a great opportunity to get direct, unedited employee views, and if it is positioned well that feedback can be targeted towards specific issues or questions that you may want to see opinion on. It is highly relevant when you want employees to have the opportunity to provide feedback or make suggestions, but without having to set up formal forums, or rely on others to facilitate the debate or transfer messages accurately from them to you.

The graffiti wall's unedited feedback can create some discomfort, so it is best used when you are able to stay open to whatever may be written or presented. Its value is short term, so you will need to be able to digest the feedback and provide responses in a short turnaround. Leaving it on the wall for too long may result in the feedback becoming stale, whilst ignoring the feedback will restrict the credibility of the process and limit future engagement with similar processes.

Best for

The graffiti wall is an all-inclusive activity – it welcomes contribution and comment from any employee, regardless of level, function or degree of involvement in the topic for discussion. It ensures that you get a broad range of perspectives, but that might also mean you see a great deal of opinion variance.

Resources

You can implement the graffiti wall idea for very little cost – some paper to cover a large wall space and some pens is all it really needs. If you have a small budget to allow for professional poster printing this may be more effective, but you could also use large rolls of paper, or whiteboard on a roll.

You should prepare your question carefully, thinking about what you want to ask for input on, and why you want feedback. Thinking retrospectively helps – when you have the feedback, what will you do with it and how will it influence your current process or thinking? If the answer is 'it won't' then it is not appropriate to ask the question.

You will need a good-sized wall space where people can gather at the poster and write/draw on it comfortably.

Outcomes

The graffiti wall will provide you with clear and unedited feedback from employees. This should be used to help you to shape your decision making, your direction or your next steps.

Process

1 Identify your key statement or question that you want feedback on – make sure that you phrase it well, so that it is clear what you are asking and what information you want to receive.
2 Prepare a 'graffiti sheet' to go on the wall, with your question in a prominent position.
3 Provide pens… and encourage people to write/draw/represent their responses to the question.
4 You may want to get a few people to start off the process – being the first can be daunting, but as the sheet fills up it gets easier.

5 Don't edit the feedback – when the graffiti wall is full, or the allocated time for feedback is up, take it away and identify the key themes from the wall. Summarize them, quoting a few examples, and ensuring that you have a good representation of all the feedback that was provided – don't just cherry pick the bits that suit you.

6 Communicate those key themes through your normal channels – team briefings, newsletters, etc – and be clear about what you will do with the feedback.

7 Prepare your next graffiti wall and repeat the process.

Hints and tips

- Be prepared – you might not like what you read. But you are capturing real views and perceptions so they are really valuable.

- Recognize that the most disengaged may not want to contribute and/or may add negative comments. Don't use this as an excuse not to do it – and resist the temptation to immediately remove it if something appears that makes you uncomfortable. Instead show the value of contribution through your actions – by collecting the responses, sharing them across the business and responding to and acting on them. This alone will encourage a more constructive participation.

- If your question is not clear or specific then your feedback is less likely to be of value. Be clear about what you want to ask, test it out on a few people first, and be prepared to provide clarification if needed.

- Acting on what you read on the wall will be the critical success factor. Like it or not, you are collecting employee opinion, so you need to respond to it pragmatically and constructively. Don't ignore it, and don't be defensive.

- Be clear about the timescales – let people know how long the wall will be active and tell them what will happen when it comes down. If people understand the timeline, and you meet the commitments, they are more likely to trust the process.

- Don't spend time trying to figure out who wrote or drew what – that is not the point and it is not a valuable way to spend your time.

  Some examples of the kind of questions you might ask are:

  - *Our recent acquisition of company X has been announced. What benefits do you think this will bring to the group?*

– *One of our values is responsibility. What does this mean for you? How can we do more to represent this value?*

– *We want our customers to LOVE us… what should we be doing to achieve that?*

Evaluation

You can evaluate the graffiti wall at three levels. Initially, looking at how much contribution has been made will give you an indication of the level of interaction employees have had with the wall. Have they felt engaged and compelled to contribute? If participation is low, this may be a factor of the communications around the approach, of the question you have asked, or your previous track record of reacting appropriately to similar feedback requests. Give it time and encourage more participation. If your wall is full of graffiti comments, the indication is that you have a good level of engagement on the topic.

The second level of evaluation is in the content itself. Consider what people are saying, asking, challenging. What does this tell you about the level of engagement with the topic, and how employees are feeling about it?

The final level is an evaluation of the reactions to your responses. Once you have reacted to the feedback, how is the organization responding to that – what are you hearing from team briefs, what actions are you seeing, how much ongoing engagement is there in the topic?

By considering all three levels of evaluation, you can evaluate not just the top level of the process, but also consider how well the intention of the process has landed in the organization.

28 Pinspiration board

The pinspiration board invites you to allocate a free noticeboard space in an open-plan office or staff relaxation area on which employees can post pictures, quotes, articles or memes that they have found interesting, relevant or motivational. These can frequently be found online, in social media or websites, and the opportunity to share, discuss and engage with them can be limited to social connections or the availability of online social media sites, which will typically only be viewed by one individual at a time. The pinspiration board provides the opportunity for some visual stimulation at work, and the opportunity to discuss it and engage with it collectively.

Similar 'tech' versions available on social media sites are considered to be really successful because of their simplicity, the freedom to post anything, and the continual stream of content. Content is shared by users for users, and in the main is not linked to a commercial requirement to buy or promote anything. Applying similar principles to the pinspiration board will help to make it a successful tool for communicating with and engaging people in your teams.

Best when

The pinspiration board is most effective in an open-plan office area or rest area in an environment where you can encourage employees to share quotes, pictures and memes that have inspired them.

Best for

Any employee should be allowed to post on the pinspiration board, but peer-to-peer content should be strongly encouraged, as opposed to management-led content.

Resources

You will need to allocate a board or wall space, but that is all. The introduction of content should be employee-led, so you don't need to invest in any posters, banners or pictures.

Making someone in the team a responsible owner, to ensure that the board is not left empty and that content is regularly refreshed, will ensure that it stays relevant.

Outcomes

The pinspiration board is intended to provide stimulating social media content to your employees via printed media on a local board. Getting teams involved may have some impact on their engagement and interaction, and the posts themselves may go some way towards providing inspiration for other colleagues.

Process

1 Set up a whiteboard or wall space in an open-plan office or coffee lounge. Make it a space that is visible to many so that it gets broad coverage and maximum impact.

2 Communicate to your teams what the whiteboard space is for – to share inspirational quotes, images, memes or ideas with fellow team members.

3 Refresh the content regularly – once content becomes old and well viewed, people will stop looking and the board will no longer be an effective tool.

4 If new content is not being posted, remind people of the purpose and the opportunity. Ultimately it may have run its course, and rather than leave an old initiative looking stale in the office, try something else for a while instead. For example, you could replace your pinspiration board with a mood board (see Section 2) or a graffiti wall (see earlier in this section).

Hints and tips

- The pinspiration board is different to your standard noticeboard, so be careful not to allow it to be taken over by health and safety notices or 'for sale' adverts. Keep its purpose clear at all times, and encourage the right type of content to be shared.

- Encouraging the right type of content is important – but equally it is intended as a peer-to-peer inspiration board. However, you may want to get the ball rolling by posting a few of your own favourites.

- There will need to be some boundaries – you will need to avoid anything that might cause offence and you will need to stay well within the bounds of your own diversity policies and, of course, equality law. As a manager, review the board regularly, remove anything that doesn't meet these criteria, and remind people about their obligations related to treatment of others in the workplace. Resist the temptation to remove the board as a result of offensive content, however – focus on addressing the behaviour, not the tool.

Evaluation

To understand how effective the pinspiration board is, review the amount of content and the different people posting content. These factors will help you to establish both the breadth and depth of engagement with the concept and intent of the board.

In addition, you might want to take a look at what themes there are in the posts from your employees. You may find that if the posts relate to a certain topic area, then it is something that is particularly relevant or meaningful for them. If this is the case, find out more and, if you are able to, take some action to address it.

29 Following the flow

Following the flow is about enabling employees to understand the process steps that happen inside your organization before and/or after the step that the employee is involved in. The employee or a team will spend time visiting the team that is responsible for the process flow prior to or immediately following their own area of activity. It allows teams or individuals to talk to each other about what they deliver or receive from each other, and to seek to build relationships, improve collaboration and improve on their own processes to the benefit of each other.

Best when

Following the flow will be most effective where there is a clear process flow or an obvious internal next step in the 'supply chain' of the organization. It can be particularly effective when there are issues, tensions or complaints between receiving and delivering departments – issues such as calls being put through to the wrong department, product quality not being adequately checked before hand-off to the next stage of the process, or systems information being incorrectly entered. By following the flow, the departments can see and understand what might cause these issues 'down' the chain, and what impact they are having further 'up'. It provides an opportunity for process improvements, more efficiency and improved hand-offs. You don't have to be having issues, though – it can work very effectively when there is no fixed agenda or predetermined problem identified, but provides a blank canvas for collaborative efforts to find improvement opportunities.

Best for

This is an effective tool for employees at all levels, in teams who are required to interact with each other on a regular basis (though not necessarily in person). It could be appropriate for managers who are open-minded about the potential opportunities it could present. This could even be considered between providers and suppliers (external to each other) if the relationship was sufficiently well established (see 'Shadowing the customer' in Section 13).

Resources

The amount of time taken for this activity will be dependent on the number of process points within the supply chain, but you could allocate anything from 30 minutes to a half-day. There is no cost for this activity, but you may need to account for the time spent, and any impact that may have on productivity. If you are looking for some process improvements as a result of this activity, be clear about the budget you may be able to allocate.

Outcomes

At the end of this exercise, the participant(s) will have an improved understanding of the feeds into and out of their own department, or part of the process. This improved understanding can lead to:

- Process improvements, particularly related to issues of quality or timeliness between the two teams.
- Collaborative suggestions – working together to solve process problems from both perspectives.
- Improved team working and elimination of silos – just by getting to know each other better, the teams may find they can empathize with problems and issues, and collaborate to jointly address them.

It is engaging because the participating employees feel that they are able to make a contribution to making improvements, and that they have had an opportunity to be heard, and to influence. It builds more effective relationships between the teams, and encourages a collaborative approach to solving problems that goes beyond the immediate activity.

Process

1 Identify the team or individual that you want to focus on for this activity.
2 Provide a briefing about their task – they are to visit the next step in the process or supply chain – that might be internal (another team or department) or external (a supplier, a distributor, a warehouse, a customer).
3 On visiting the next-step team, the individual or group should:
   - Take time to understand the process flow in that department – what happens when, who has what responsibilities, etc.
   - Understand where and how their own work connects to that of the department they are visiting.
   - Explore with the hosting team the opportunities there may be for improvement – identify one or two things that would make things better/faster/cheaper/easier for both teams. Ask questions like:

- What do you need from me to ensure the best quality?
- What could we do that would help to speed up your process?
- Are we double-handling or repeating processes?
- What would enable a smooth handover of product/process from one team to another?

4 The two teams should take the opportunity to work out one or two manageable solutions between themselves.

5 Ideally the team will be empowered to implement the solutions or ideas that they identify. If not they should be encouraged to bring their solutions back as proposals for approval by a senior team.

Hints and tips

- Repeat the process moving forwards or backwards in the supply/process chain, but focus each team on their neighbours in the process flow.
- Share the success stories from this activity more widely in the organization. This could encourage greater participation.

Evaluation

In evaluating its success, gauge the interaction between the departments – is it more or less? Is it of a more constructive nature? Are the teams collaborating?

Identify whether there have been any process improvements – and what additional benefits they have had on your cost, quality, efficiency, etc.

In talent attraction 04

30 Compelling brand

The CIPD Employer Brand factsheet (CIPD, 2016c) defines an employer brand as 'a set of attributes and qualities, often intangible, that makes an organization distinctive, promises a particular kind of employment experience, and appeals to those people who will thrive and perform best in its culture', and states that to be effective it must 'connect an organization's values, people strategy and HR policies and be linked to the company brand'.

Within the context of engagement, and particularly of engaging a very broad audience during talent attraction, the compelling brand seeks to engage an external audience (in parallel with the internal audience) with a view to promoting to them your organization as an aspirational employer, as a place where they want to work.

In developing the compelling brand it is critical to be transparent about your company aims, values and opportunities if you are to encourage applications from those candidates who feel an affinity with those things. Sharing and promoting stories that demonstrate those aims, values and opportunities will build your compelling brand and begin to engage your audience.

Best when

A compelling brand can be an extremely useful tool for you to use to build your reputation as an employer when recruiting external candidates into your organization. However, to build a strong reputation, and to create a story that will be of interest to future potential candidates, this needs to be an ongoing activity. The brand will need to be maintained, stories updated, and feedback responded to. The brand must have a sense of permanency – this is not an aspect of the organization that should change frequently. Ideally, when a new employee starts in your organization they will recognize the brand values that were promoted during their recruitment campaign, and they will continue to see them evidenced (not just hear them discussed) over the course of their career. Of course the brand will be adapted, but just as you continue to recognize major consumer goods brands as they change over time (like a can of Coca-Cola, for example) the brand should remain true to its core identity through those changes.

Best for

It is possible to engage all of your workforce in promoting your brand as an employer. However, you may want to take care that you – or a nominated person – remain in control of messaging to and feedback from a public audience. In reality, the more your external employer brand messaging comes from advocates across your business, the more engaging it will be to your chosen audience. It will make a bigger impact than messages that are considered to be 'corporate'.

Resources

There are two ways to approach the compelling brand. One is to invest in branding and marketing support from specialist agencies and consultancies in order to build and promote your employer brand. Specialist agencies will be able to help you to develop the brand, in line with your external product or service branding and your core values. They will define with you the important attributes of the organization and its people, the selling points that will attract candidates, and the stories behind your employer brand – for employee case studies that provide personal experiences of progression, or demonstrating the values through the work that they do. This of course would require financial investment, and most likely you would have to be able to demonstrate that there will be a clear return on that investment.

The other way is to create the brand, the rationale behind the brand and the case studies, and allow the brand to build itself. You will need to allocate a resource from inside your organization to take a lead role in doing this, and may need a supporting team, but unless your organization is very large, these are not tasks that require dedicated resource.

Because many of your compelling brand initiatives can be implemented through the use of social media, you do not necessarily need to allocate a significant budget. Setting aside some funds may allow you the opportunity to do a little more, or to be more creative, and so is worth consideration.

Outcomes

By promoting your business as a good employer, a story supported by advocates from your existing workforce, you are aiming to engage an external audience. That audience may well include some potential future candidates for and employees in your business. This early engagement of the audience is an important part of talent attraction. A survey by Gallup has shown that: 'High-quality job candidates are attracted to companies that align with who they are and encourage them to do what they do best... choose to work for companies that match who they are and what they believe in... that present them with opportunities to fully apply their skills' (Houle and Campbell, 2016). In contrast, lower-quality candidates were attracted to pay, benefits, hours of work, etc.

Process

1 Identify an individual in your organization who will take overall accountability for the compelling brand initiative. If your organization employs a marketing specialist or a marketing team, their expertise will be invaluable through the development and utilization of the brand. Ensure they are well briefed and have clarity about the objectives and deliverables or outcomes that are expected.

2 Using existing company documentation, such as your business strategy, goals and values statements, supported by informal discussions or focus groups with your employees (a dialogue sheet could work really well for this activity – see Section 2), start to build a series of statements about or foundations for your compelling employer brand. You may need to break this down into different elements for different segments of your workforce.

3 Once you have your compelling employer brand proposal, test it with your internal audience – from the leadership team to the shop floor – to see that it resonates, that it is realistic and it communicates effectively with the desired messages landing well with an audience. Adjust as necessary based on the feedback you receive, and get sign-off from your business leaders for your proposition.

4 Your next step is to consider how to move from the statements on the page to then bringing that compelling brand to life. Capturing case studies, stories, videos, photographs of events, and soundbites and feedback from customers, suppliers, employees, leaders and other stakeholders will

all add to a portfolio of evidence that can be used to promote your brand. Make sure you have permission to use images and quotes from those who made/feature in them.

5 Use social media as a fast, efficient and effective way to promote the compelling brand, but do be aware of the risks associated. Consider in advance how you might deal with negative responses to your campaign.

6 Plan the first phase of the campaign in detail – what you will promote, and when and where. Consider who has sign-off on the final wording of any posts or notices, and who will manage responses and reactions as they come in. Be cautious to start with. The audience will notice if you start with a great deal of activity and it slowly tails off. It is better to have a regular heartbeat of activity, at a pace that you can maintain on an ongoing basis. Consider too the variety of media that you might use – across different social media platforms, as well as through your own internal communications media (for more ideas see 'Communicate, communicate, communicate' in Section 2).

7 Review the effectiveness of your campaign, make any changes to improve it based on your experience to date and plan your next phase.

Hints and tips

- Don't forget to revisit – and if necessary update – your social media policy. It may need to reflect your compelling brand initiative, associated responsibilities, and what can and cannot be in the public domain.

- Do not ignore your internal audience – make sure that the messages communicated through your compelling brand campaign are shared internally too.

- Check for alignment. Do your organizational culture, your ways of working, your policies and procedures and what happens in practice all truly line up with the compelling brand you have developed? Being transparent is important, and being true to your organization is too. If your organization prides itself on innovation and creativity, then that should be reflected in your brand. But if your organization prides itself on compliance, accuracy and detail, then that is what should be reflected. Don't pick the trendy words and phrases because you think they will resonate better to an external audience – pick the ones that really represent your business.

- Search the internet for 'employer brand examples' and you will see some great examples from companies that you know well – but avoid the copy-and-paste approach – you need to consider the points above in order to really make your brand work for you.

Evaluation

There are a number of dimensions under which the success of a compelling brand can be evaluated. These include, but are not limited to:

- Employee connection: are your own employees connecting with the branding? Are they participating in campaigns actively (offering stories, posting photographs, etc) or passively (liking and sharing information on social media)?

- External brand engagement: are external audiences engaging with the campaigning, commenting, liking, sharing posts and campaign materials? Are you capturing that audience, by connecting with individuals, responding and thanking them, etc?

- Applicant and candidate engagement: more specifically, are you attracting potential candidates for new positions? What impact is the campaign having on your advertising methods and response rates?

- Quality and commitment of new starters: are you able to select a higher quality of candidate? Are you retaining more new starters rather than seeing them leave early on in their employment with you? Is overall turnover reducing?

31 Inclusive selection

To facilitate buy-in and commitment to the selection of a new starter, use inclusive selection processes that allow for informal but valuable 'meet and greet' between candidates and potential future peers. Whilst these processes provide a great opportunity for a 'meet and greet' of preferred candidates, it can also provide second, third, or more, perspectives on those candidates.

Best when

This is at its most effective when you have shortlisted your candidates to a final stage of the selection process. Introducing it too early in the selection process is likely to take up a great deal of time, much of which may be wasted on candidates who are unlikely to be successful. Involving others too late (ie when you have selected your preferred candidate) may appear to be paying lip service to the initiative, or, if the peer group is very influential, this may mean you have to start the process from scratch.

Best for

Whilst this can be done at all levels in the organization it is mostly likely to be effective, and valuable, when recruiting to management and senior roles where a multistage process is more common. However, you should also bear in mind the capability of the peers to objectively and fairly assess candidates based on an informal interaction.

Resources

There is no direct cost for this activity, but you may have to factor the time taken for future peers to attend, and travel expenses for your candidate. You will need a good meeting room and some hospitality (a buffet lunch or breakfast, or some teas and coffees).

Outcomes

Engaging with this process should ensure that your managers feel a greater sense of engagement with selection decisions, and that the selection of candidates is in the main supported by their peers. Ideally this means that when on-boarding new starters, you will get good support from their peers in induction, and accelerating the building of the new team, as the new starter will not be a stranger.

Process

1 Identify the colleagues who you would like to meet the candidates – ideally peers and key stakeholders with whom they may interface in the new role. They may be more senior, but it is unlikely that at this stage you would involve more junior participants, or those who would be managed by the new starter.

2 Brief the colleagues about their role in the meet and greet – clarify the roles that each person will play in the session and be clear about your expectations. Typically this might include, for example:

Consider the following in your discussions and summations:

- Chemistry: the person in this role will sit with you as a peer on your team. Could you see yourself working effectively with them? What strengths will they add to the team? What difference do they bring that could be effective?

- Culture fit: what are your views about how the candidates might fit into the working environment, culture and ways of working?

- Challenges: do they have relevant, advantageous, transferable experience that will enable them to support the team's goals and challenges, as well as those of the company as a whole?

3 Ask colleagues to do a little prep work to prepare some informal, conversational questions about candidate background and experience and the future expectations of the role. Consider whether you want to provide them with the candidate CVs, or whether you would prefer them to go into the session and have to find out information via discussion. If you choose for them not to see the CV, make sure the candidates know that this is the approach – or they may assume that no one did their homework!

4 This is not positioned as a panel interview, but rather an informal 'meet and greet', so the feel of the session should be informal and conversational, not interrogative.

5 It is also the candidates' opportunity to make the same assessment – do they want to work with you and are the challenges you present of interest to them? To this end, future peers should encourage questions.

6 Future peers will not be expected to provide scoring or rating of the candidate but their feedback should be considered in the context of formal interview and selection criteria and outcomes.

Hints and tips

- Brief candidates (and/or agencies) on what to expect in this process. It would be unfair to surprise the candidate with this session. Make sure that they know in advance who they will be meeting (and how many people).

- Keep it informal – include a buffet breakfast/lunch or tea and biscuits.

- Give someone a lead or buddy role to keep the conversation flowing, keep the people circulating and keep the timing on track.

- Bear in mind the potential risks of this process. If you go ahead and recruit a candidate who was not preferred by some or all of your peers, you risk the opposite of your desired outcome – that the new starter will not be warmly welcomed, and that the team will not bond quickly. You will need to ensure that you listen to feedback from the peer group, and that you are able to explain your rationale for selection despite their comments. You may not always be able to satisfy everyone's preferences, but their understanding of the selection decision may be an important factor in acceptance.

Evaluation

Given that the primary purpose of this activity is to encourage the involvement and feedback of future peers in the recruitment and selection process, this should be your first level of evaluation for this exercise. Ask:

- Were future peers willing participants in the process?

- Did they provide constructive feedback on the candidate, based on the briefing that you had provided to them?

- Did they enjoy meeting the candidates and participating in the process?

At a secondary level, it is useful to consider whether peer involvement influenced the process:

- Was their preferred candidate selected? If not, why not?

- Was their feedback used to shape further stages of the selection process – eg did you ask any additional questions as a result of feedback received from future peers?

- Did their feedback influence the selection decision?

Finally, it is useful to consider whether peer involvement in the selection decision had any impact on the on-boarding process:

- Did the new starter feel warmly welcomed?

- Did the team bond and begin to work together quickly?

In induction 05

The 'hello' hamper

The 'hello' hamper is a box of important information and treats to give to new employees when they arrive. At a very basic level, it provides new starters with some of the things they need to get started in the role, but can also provide some extras too that demonstrate that you have given consideration to their needs as a person, not just as a new resource. It is intended to create a warm welcome for the new starter, and create a positive impression of the company, the team and the boss on the first day.

Best when

This is an initiative for a new employee's first day at work. Have it ready and on their workspace on their first day, in time for their arrival. This may take some planning, so get started early, don't leave it until the last minute to think about it.

Best for

This is best for new employees only. You would not normally include existing employees who transfer, as they should have all the information and goodies that you include. However, if you choose to give this to transfers, make sure that the content is relevant to someone who has already been in the organization for some time.

Resources

It will take a small amount of time to prepare it (some shopping and preparation time).

You can set a budget for your hello hamper, but don't assume this has to be expensive. It can be as effective with a small budget as it would with a significant one.

You will need a willing volunteer to prepare the hamper – it could be a good idea for this person to be the new starter's 'buddy'. You will also need some standard company information, such as employee handbooks, key policies and procedures. Check with your HR specialist as to what might be included.

Outcomes

The hello hamper is intended to get your new joiner engaged early, and feel valued from the very beginning. It is engaging because by demonstrating that you have thought about them in advance, you are giving an indication that your employees do matter to your business. Your preparation also gives consideration to their needs in their first few days – some key information for example – as well as treats.

Process

1 Buy and/or prepare the hamper contents.

2 Fill the hamper with the items you have collected.

3 Leave it – with a welcoming note from you and/or their new team – on the new joiner's new desk ready for their first day!

Hints and tips

- Make sure it is on the new starter's desk or workspace before they arrive – if items are missing, forget them and put it in place anyway. You don't want to look disorganized on day one!

- This is not actually about spending a big budget. It would be great to include a magnum of champagne, but the important message here is that you were ready, you were thinking about the joiner, you wanted to offer them a warm welcome. So keep the contents realistic against the backdrop of your business.

- Providing some logo/promotional materials might be beneficial, but don't make it all about that – a mix of those materials (to create a sense of belonging) and other treats (to create a sense of value) will be beneficial.

- Please don't leave your new joiner alone on day one to sift through their hamper – keeping them active, engaged and social on day one with the manager, the team and a buddy will make a big difference to how someone feels about their new job at the end of their first day or week.

- Some things you might include:
  - Low budget:
    - bag of sweets;
    - pens;

- notebook (daybook);
- bottle of wine;
- coffee-shop card – preloaded with £5;
- mints;
- logo goods – a mug/mousemat;
- your company handbook;
- important policies;
- social activities information;
- lunch menus;
- organization charts;
- newsletters.
- Bigger budget:
  - champagne;
  - chocolates;
  - notebooks;
  - pens;
  - coffee-shop card – preloaded with £10–20;
  - cinema voucher;
  - phone charger;
  - logo goods – a mug/brolly/mousemat/T-shirt;
  - laptop bag;
  - your company handbook;
  - important policies;
  - social activities information;
  - lunch menus;
  - organization charts;
  - newsletters.

Evaluation

- What was the new employee's reaction?
- What feedback do you get about 'first day' processes?

33 Enablement plan

Enablement ensures that an employee has everything they need in order to be effective in their work. This could be as simple as equipment, machinery, supplies, access to systems, a password, etc – or it could go as far as skills and knowledge provided through training, contacts and networks, or knowing the delivery expectations. A fully enabled employee can operate effectively without close supervision, as they are provided with everything they need in order to perform.

Enablement is an ongoing issue not a one-off intervention, but the preparation of a sound enablement plan can have a significant impact on the integration of a new employee to your business.

An enablement plan ensures that employees have the skills, knowledge and experience, as well as the equipment, tools and materials that they need to do their job well. When combined with high levels of employee engagement, you can expect high levels of employee effectiveness.

Best when

Enablement is most effective when implementation is started prior to the new starter's first day with you, and some actions that may continue into their induction period and beyond. This may take some time to plan and implement, so early initiation will be beneficial. The engagement plan is both a precursor to and a supporting document for induction planning.

Best for

This tool is all about helping new starters to settle into your organization and to be quickly able to perform. Whilst the enablement tool is beneficial for all, individual requirements may differ. Consideration should be given to the different needs of different individuals, different roles, functions, and levels of experience and seniority.

Resources

The resources required for the enablement plan will be dependent on the activity required. Be prepared to set aside some funding and allocate time for travel arrangements, training needs, and ensuring that equipment and materials are readily available.

Outcomes

Enablement is an important part of the new starter process. Its intention is to accelerate the induction period, in which newly appointed employees can often feel that they are not equipped to quickly add value. In addition to enabling them to add value, a good enablement plan will demonstrate to the new employee that their arrival is eagerly expected, that their needs have been considered and that their ability to settle in is a priority for you as their line manager.

Process

1 Consider the needs of your new starter by completing an engagement plan template (see Table 5.1) for each individual. Adapt the template as you need to for the individual, the job or the team, and ensure that the enablement plan covers the requirements of all aspects of the job.

2 Ask your existing team members to review your plan. Particularly helpful in this cross-check are your most recent starters – having been through the induction process themselves, they may have some useful insights about what could be included in an individual plan.

3 Implement the enablement plan.

4 Review with the new starter on a weekly basis during their first three months to ensure that progress is being made.

Hints and tips

Whilst some elements of the engagement plan could be transferrable for the same jobs across the organization, it is not advisable to copy and paste for every new starter. The enablement plan should be bespoke and based on individual needs and requirements.

Table 5.1   Enablement plan template

Employee details
Employee name
Start date
Job title
Department
Function

(continued)

Table 5.1   *(Continued)*

Knowledge, skills and experience
What company or job-specific skills are required that the new starter will not have on joining?
How might these needs be met during the first three months?
What follow-up might be required?

Tools/equipment
What tools or equipment (including IT) are required for the job?

Materials/stationery
What materials or stationery are required for the job?
Other Important factors
What else does the new starter NEED to know?
What else would it be good for the new starter to learn?

Evaluation

There are two areas of focus for enablement – individual and organizational:

- Individual: here the primary concern is the effect that the enablement plan had on the employee. It is mostly concerned with their temperament and attitude towards the development and actioning of the plan and will require you to ask questions of the new starter such as:

- Did you have all the equipment and information you needed when you started?
- What worked well/what else do you need?
- Was there anything missing or unexpected?
- In addition you could consider adopting a 'happy sheet'-style questionnaire to gather feedback (an example is provided in Table 16.2 at the back of this book).

- Organizational: here the focus is on the effect that the enablement plan had on the organization, by assessing how quickly the individual was able to add value and contribute to overall team or functional performance. As the manager you are more likely to be able to assess these points for yourself. Ask yourself questions such as:

- How quickly was the new starter adding value in the team?
- What information or equipment helped to speed up the induction process?
- What else could help?
- What feedback have you received?

In training   06

Chew and chat

Chew and chat is an opportunity for an informal communications session, Q&A or short training intervention with a group of voluntary attendees. This is typically not compulsory – it is during a lunch break and so should be positioned as an optional attendance. It is usually a short 30–45 minute session, which should allow people to take a break from work, eat their lunch whilst in the session with you, and benefit from some informal learning or information.

Best when

Chew and chat is a great opportunity to build some relationships with teams, particularly because the attendees are willing volunteers. It is extremely beneficial when the organization or team are going though change, or experiencing difficult market conditions, because it allows for regular informal discussions. The lead for each session needs to be competent and comfortable in delivering informally, without script or slides to depend on.

Best for

Typically, chew and chat offers the advantage of having a positively engaged audience from the start. It should therefore be open to anyone to attend – and as it is taking place during an allocated lunch break, and the content is informal, there should be no reason to deny anyone the chance to participate.

Resources

Chew and chat requires no real investment other than a space to meet up, and a speaker for the session. You may want to advertise or promote the session internally, but costs are minimal. Where cost is not a barrier, or where you can demonstrate a clear return on investment, an external speaker or trainer could add value and suggest a level of credibility to the process but will require a reasonable budget to be set. Be careful, though, not to start with a 'big bang' that sets expectations that cannot be maintained.

Outcomes

The intended outcome of your chew and chat session will depend on the content and objective you set for each one. However, the generic intention of it as an engagement tool is that it brings together people from across your organization, regardless of seniority, function or responsibility, and places them on a level playing field to learn or share something new. This in itself promotes learning, it fosters communication and it breaks down silos. The specific content for each will bring its own benefits as added value too.

Process

1 Establish a series of chew and chat events over a period of time (eg one per month for six months), and use each session slightly differently.

2 Provide an opportunity to attend – if your attendance is not limited by size of venue, then just ask people to turn up. By doing so, you establish chew and chat as a forum for almost anything, rather than as the 'communications forum' or a 'training session'. Mixing up the content and purpose will keep people's interest – and people who choose not to attend one format may well choose to attend something different.

3 If you need to limit numbers based on venue capacity, find an informal way to encourage people to sign up – eg a note and volunteer sheet in the rest room, or a waiting list on the meeting-room door.

4 Use your standard communications media to promote the chew and chat session, and remind people that it is informal, a one-off, and an 'eat and greet' session – bring your own lunch!

5 Don't make this action-oriented, the target is to bring people together for discussion or learning. If they feel that tasks or actions may be allocated, participation may decline.

Hints and tips

There are a few categories you could consider for chew and chat:

- Open Q&A: the lead for the chew and chat session must be well briefed and competent to deliver clear and open communications. An open Q&A

session can stray into many areas of discussion and debate and you will need to ensure that the lead in the session knows the opportunities and the limitations of the session. You might find media training (see Section 2) helpful in preparation (see also 'Top team unplugged' in Section 3).

- Discussion topics: you may choose to set an open topic for discussion for the chew and chat, for example: 'How can we build customer loyalty?' 'Do we really know our customers?' 'How can we deliver an improved customer experience?' It is advisable to stay away from topics that suggest things are wrong – pick a topic that focuses on the positives or opportunities rather than on fixing problems. By setting a talking topic you can guide the conversation – but the leader should still prepare – giving some thought to questions that might guide the debate. As the leader, though, it may be useful to consider some key takeaways and what you might do with them.

- Training sessions: if you are using chew and chat as a training session, keep the content short, focused and interactive – preferably without slides. See 'Light bites' later in this section for some ideas.

- Non-work interests: consider using the chew and chat model occasionally for non-work interests. For example, if you have employees with specific hobbies, interests or charity connections, they could run sessions themselves to promote or engage people in those. Whilst not directly impacting your business, this could build interaction, communication and teamwork, and may create a positive reputation around the chew and chat concept that encourages greater participation.

Evaluation

Given the variety of topic areas available to you through chew and chat, one of the key indicators will be the level of engagement that people feel in the process on that day. Completion of the basic 'happy sheet' evaluations (Did you enjoy it? What would you like more of? etc) will provide some evaluation of the value of the content for the participants.

Overall, consider the number of people who sign up and compare this with the number attending in order to provide an indication of how well received the concept is, how 'enabled' people feel to attend (instead of working through lunch) and how attractive the content is to them at face value.

35 Light bites

Light bites is an approach to learning that is based on the 'Pomodoro' technique developed by Cirillo (2006). Cirillo proposed a method of breaking down work into 'Pomodoros' of 25 minutes, with short breaks in between. He based this approach on the idea that mental agility can be improved with frequent breaks, with an ideal Pomodoro of 25–30 minutes long, 40 minutes maximum.

This was the main influence behind the light bites concept. Focusing on developing short, sharp training content recognizes Cirillo's theory that agility is improved – or at least more focused – in that time. It seems logical to incorporate this as a strong influence in training design, limiting modules to short, sharp concepts or topics in just one 'Pomodoro'.

Research by the Institute of Employment Studies (Robinson, Perryman and Hayday, 2004) suggests that one factor that influences how engaged employees are is the opportunity to develop their jobs, and involvement in training, development and career plans.

This suggests that the provision of relevant training across the organization could have a positive impact on employee engagement, but often the barrier to that is cost. The light bites approach could enable low-cost, internally driven, regular training events to take place, supporting the learning objectives of many within the organization.

> 'Train people well enough so they can leave, treat them well enough so they don't want to.'
>
> *Richard Branson*

Best when

Light bites works effectively when the company is keen to offer training and development opportunities, but has limited time and budget and/or the reputation of training programmes has faltered. By breaking training into manageable chunks, participants will not be overloaded with new learnings, but can identify key takeaways and put them into practice straight away.

Best for

Light bites can be available for all employees, but you may find that certain topics attract specific functions or levels of seniority. Your advertising should make it clear, however, that there is no eligibility criteria, and that anyone can attend any topic.

Resources

The light bites modules can be delivered in-house, at minimal cost, or you could bring in external providers to design and/or deliver the content for you. Because they are short sessions, they are usually accommodated in-house, in a low-tech manner with no need for refreshments. Of course you could run them in a high-tech way with plenty of refreshments too! Essentially, light bites modules do not need heavy investment of money, but they may take some time to design effectively and to deliver. Bear in mind that if you use internal resources to do this, you take them away from their day job.

Outcomes

Developing the skills of your employees not only ensures that you are building engagement, but also that you develop their capabilities, building on your talent base for the future of your organization. Engaging internal resources to design and deliver light bites modules can also increase their perception of value within the organization, as well as adding a new skill to their own portfolio.

Process

1 Identify some topic areas for relevant training in your business. Break down these topic areas into the smallest possible module headings, and focus in on each to design and deliver a 25-minute interactive speed-learning session.

2 Encourage support from across the organization to design and deliver the light bites modules. If your organization has 'technical' experts, encourage them to design and deliver a session. Make sure that any trainers or presenters are well trained, and briefed as to the approach that light bites takes. Overrunning, or expecting significant break-out discussions, etc, will not be very practical, and may be better served through a more traditional training programme.

3 Delivering a broad range of content will be important if you want to encourage maximum participation.

4 There may be some content that is mandatory – you may choose to deliver these through a light bites session (eg health and safety, diversity and inclusion, induction, etc).

5 Some modules can be delivered in person, others could be delivered by e-learning or through self-learning PowerPoint presentations. Consider the content, and the level of interaction that would be beneficial, when determining how to deliver the module. If you have people working remotely (across sites or from home) a webinar can be an effective way of delivering short modules through light bites.

6 End each module with two or three key takeaways – the main soundbites that you want participants to remember and focus on. Keep them short, punchy, memorable and relevant.

Hints and tips

Some examples of topics covered in light bites modules include:

- motivating others;
- customer service;
- using powerful questions;
- health and safety;
- product-knowledge modules;
- know your customer.

Evaluation

Completion of the basic 'happy sheet' evaluations (Did you enjoy it? What would you like more of? etc) will provide some evaluation of the value of the content for the participants.

Overall, consider the number of people who participate in order to give an indication of how well received the topic is, and how 'enabled' people feel to attend.

36 Communities of practice

'Community organizing is all about building grass-roots support. It is about identifying the people around you with whom you can create a common, passionate cause.'

Tom Peters

A community of practice brings together groups of employees with specific interests, and encourages them to learn and develop through regular inter-action that promotes the sharing of knowledge, expertise and experience. The community is connected by the interest itself, which in your workplace might be a technically specialist capability, or an interest area such as lead-ership, mindfulness, change management or communications. Its members do not have to be closely associated in their work, they may be functionally or geographically spread, but they will meet regularly to engage in discus-sion about the specialist interest. This discussion – and the collaborative approach to sharing experiences and stories, and the collective problem-solving and practitioner expertise – leads to the continued development of the specialist interest.

Good examples of communities of practice are often found on the inter-net, or through social media forums and chat rooms, where users who may not be connected in normal daily life are able to discuss and share expertise on specific areas of interest through a virtual community, typically sharing information, articles, news topics and chat.

In many organizations the communities can be organized as face-to-face activities. However, if your employees are geographically dispersed, you may want to consider how you can use technology to establish a virtual community and achieve the same goals.

Best when

The community of practice can be extremely useful to your organization. Promoting and advocating continuous development, it helps to embed a learning culture and enables the development of specialist interest areas, but without having to commit to a significant financial commitment. With this in mind, establishing and supporting a community of practice in an interest that is of importance and priority to your business will be valuable to you.

Best for

The community of practice is aimed specifically at those employees with specific interests in which you want to encourage continuous learning, development and collaboration. It may be function-specific, though this is not a prerequisite as the specialist interests may span a range of functions or technical areas. Suitable for employees at all levels in the organization, this is likely to be most effective in larger organizations, where the community will be large enough to foster learnings from other members.

Resources

The community of practice does not need a significant budget. Participants may need a meeting place (on- or off-site), and if your organization is geographically dispersed they may need some travel budget.

Whilst the primary source of learning is to develop participant knowledge through the building of their own community, it could be beneficial to include formal training interventions occasionally. However, there should be no commitment to this – once you have committed, you have to deliver, so keeping it as an occasional ad hoc decision would be better.

You might want to consider setting aside a small budget for incidentals such as food and drink for meetings, etc.

Outcomes

The community of practice is intended to engage its members by establishing close associations among employees with common specialist interests. Company support for the community of practice initiative demonstrates an interest in developing the skills and specialisms of members. From a company perspective, the community of practice enables the development of skills and capabilities in those special interest areas that are promoted, and builds collaboration across the organization. This may ultimately have an impact on what or how you deliver in your business, and a community of employees who have influenced that are likely to feel more engaged at work.

Process

1 Establish the specialist interest communities that your organization would be keen to promote. These might be based on your business strategy,

specific focus areas for the coming 12–24 months or social responsibility projects that you want to undertake, for example.

2 Design the mandate and scope for the community. What are the objectives of establishing the community, and what outcomes do you expect from the group? Decide how many members can be invited to participate, and set out some of the guidelines for how the group might operate (eg frequency of meeting, methods of interaction, etc).

3 Communicate your intention to establish the community of practice. Explain the objectives, the benefits of being a member and how membership will be decided.

4 Invite potential members to join the community. You may want to consider whether a selection process is useful, or whether anyone who shares the interest can join. If you do utilize a selection process, give some thought to what might be the 'entry qualifications' to join the community.

5 Plan a facilitated kick-off meeting that helps the community to define in more detail:

   – Our purpose:
      – Why have we been brought together as a community of practice? What value can we add – to the business, to each other, to ourselves? How is the community of practice aligned to the business strategy? How long is our lifespan anticipated to be?

   – Our deliverables:
      – What will success look like? How will we evaluate our performance/contribution as a community?

   – Our development:
      – How will we promote and demonstrate learning in our community? What resources/connections/access do we need internally and externally to facilitate that?

   – Our process:
      – When will we meet? Where will we meet? What roles do we have in the team for organizing, communicating, etc?

6 Allow the community to run. Consider whether you want to see outputs and deliverables from the community and, if you do, make sure your expectations are clear. If you are asking the community to deliver something specific, set the milestones with the participants and agree the approach for reporting back.

7 Encourage the community to make use of tools such as light bites (see earlier in this section) and chew and chat (see earlier in this section) to share their own knowledge and findings across the organization. You could try community unplugged, using a similar approach to the top team unplugged (see Section 3).

8 Ensure that the community of practice has a finite end. You may establish this at the start of the process, or it might become apparent that the community has served its purpose after a period of time. Either way, don't allow the community of practice to merely drift away. Instead, formally mark the closure with a workshop or meeting at which the community can:

- celebrate their progress, noting the new knowledge, findings, ideas, etc;
- mark successes that are connected to business deliverables;
- identify some personal growth highlights;
- agree how to keep valuable connections live.

Hints and tips

- Encourage the community to utilize some of the idea- and inspiration-generating tools from this book – particularly hot topics (see Section 2) and inspiring cinema club (see Section 3) – through the course of their meetings.

- It may be beneficial to allocate a facilitator to the community to encourage them to seek value in each meeting. This could be an internal specialist or an external provider. Or you may have a facilitation community of practice that you can draw on!

Evaluation

The evaluation of the success of a community of practice can be done at a number of levels. At its most basic level is the assessment of whether the members of the community have enjoyed the experience, have found value in being a member, and feel they have learned something new from their participation. A simple happy sheet will provide this information for your evaluation (an example is provided in Table 16.2 at the end of this book).

You can also evaluate the success of the community of practice against the scope it set for itself, from simply considering whether it met as frequently as intended, whether participation was good from members, to whether they met the established objectives.

However, it is important to capture the overriding purpose of the community of practice in your evaluation, and this may require a deeper assessment of its impact. Consider the following questions as a starting point:

- Has the community had any influence on the business strategy (*what* is being delivered) or its implementation (*how* it is being delivered)?

- Has the community developed the knowledge/awareness/skill of the wider organization in its specialist area?

When life changes happen 07

37 Keep in touch

Keep-in-touch days (known as KIT), typically used by employees whilst an employee is absent on maternity leave, provide the opportunity for an employee to remain in contact and attend the workplace during their extended absence.

The keep-in-touch approach recommends that during periods of long or regular intermittent absence you continue to engage team members through regular calls, writing, inviting and ensuring that they share company news, important information and team updates.

You may think that as they are not at work you don't need to invest time in them – after all you will not see a return on that investment in the short term – or that you should leave them in peace and provide them with a well-intentioned break from work. However, consider how it might feel if you were absent for a period, whether planned or unexpectedly, and no one from work made contact with you. You may feel isolated, forgotten or unimportant. The intent with keep in touch is to promote the opposite feelings so that those employees who are absent still feel included as part of the team, and an important member of it. This will be even more important in helping them to resettle on their return.

Best for

As already mentioned, keep-in-touch (KIT) days are typically used by employees whilst an employee is absent on maternity leave. However, there can be a great many reasons why KIT days might be beneficial to others. This tool sits under the heading of life changes. As well as becoming a new parent (connecting KIT to maternity, paternity and adoption leave) we now could consider the addition of grandparent leave, bereavement, a period of long-term illness, or several periods of shorter-term absence for a known and managed condition. Employees on secondment or working overseas for extended periods might also be considered for the KIT approach.

Best when

The timing for a KIT day will depend on the reason for absence, and on any important triggers or events back in the business.

Resources

This a low-resource initiative. It takes only your time, so the direct cost of keeping in touch is negligible.

Outcomes

Absent employees should continue to feel engaged during their time away from work – they should not be made to feel isolated, or that those back at the workplace have forgotten them or don't care. KIT days provide the mechanism for that engagement to continue during absence, and act as a reminder to stay inclusive.

Process

1 When a person takes longer-term leave from your business, immediately check in with them about your intention to keep in touch and agree the best methodology (call, e-mail, visits, etc) and confirm their contact details.

2 Agree your approach to keep in touch – it is better that the employee knows what to expect from you during their absence, and what their own responsibilities are with regards to maintaining contact. Managing expectations means that the employee is more likely to have a positive reaction to your KIT plans, rather than feeling concerned that you are not allowing them the space that they need.

3 Note down any key trigger points – it might be useful to diarize them – to keep in touch with your employee. For example, after important company meetings, team events, announcements. Alternatively they may be driven by the employees' issues – eg after an important appointment, a funeral or having a baby.

4 Ensure that you make regular contact, respond to the triggers identified and remain inclusive in your communications approach. E-mail minutes of important meetings and, if it is appropriate, continue to invite your absent employee to major events and social activities. They can, of course, choose whether to attend, but the simple act of extending the invitation is likely to foster engagement.

Hints and tips

- Under maternity and adoption it is entirely voluntary to attend work for a KIT day, but an employee can work up to 10 KIT days during their leave. The Advisory, Conciliation and Arbitration Service (ACAS) offers guidelines about KIT days during maternity leave.

- Use this approach in conjunction with your leave and absence policies.

- There is a fine line between keeping engaged and hassling people back to work. It is best to keep the KIT days separate to any formal processes for managing an employee's absence.

- When you are wondering about whether you should keep in touch, consider how you might like to be treated. Being left alone might feel like being ignored, and so by making occasional contact you not only help to keep the employee involved and help them be ready to return at the right time, you also show a human interest in your team member, demonstrating that they are not forgotten, they are missed, and they are still valuable to you and their colleagues.

Evaluation

Gathering employee feedback will be the most effective form of evaluation for KIT days. Whilst you can consider a simple metric (eg how many KIT days were utilized during an absence period) this will only give you a quantitative evaluation. Asking for qualitative feedback will be more useful in assessing the value of KIT days, and in giving guidance about how to improve your approach to them.

When career changes happen 08

At the beginning of this book the importance of both engagement and enablement was described in creating highly effective employees. Whilst this might be more easily remembered at the point of induction of a new starter, it can often be forgotten for those who transfer between teams, departments or functions. In the next two tools the focus is on how to ensure that the transferee is re-engaged and re-enabled, in order to bring them back to optimum effectiveness as quickly as possible during their transition.

38 Re-engage

Re-engaging the employee at the point of their transfer from one department, function or internal company is important to ensure that they understand the common ground and the key differences from their previous job, team, department and business unit. The transferee should be encouraged to bring their knowledge, skills and experience with them, but also to recognize what may be different, and begin to adapt to it.

This is more than just an induction plan. The induction plan will still be important in helping the transferred employee to get on with the job and build relationships with their new team and new stakeholders. However, re-engaging them is about more than that – it is about ensuring that they can make new connections about why they do what they do in this new role.

Best for

Re-engagement is targeted at employees who are transferring from one role to another. Whether that transfer requires them to change function, business unit, geography, etc will only influence how much re-engagement is required.

Best when

It is important to plan the activities to support re-engagement prior to the employee's start date in your part of the business. They should have the opportunity to quickly and proactively reconnect with the business in this different context, and delaying any activities may delay the speed with which they can begin to add value.

Resources

The re-engagement activities will take time to plan, and time from yourself and other key stakeholders to implement. Dependent on the activities that you want to include in re-engagement, you may need to allocate some budget for travel expenses and any incidentals.

Outcomes

The primary intention for re-engagement is that transferred employees quickly feel reconnected to the business, and can relate to their new role and understand its impact on the overall goals of the function or organization. It is intended that the transferee is able to understand what is different from their previous position, and how they can make a difference to results and deliverables.

Process

You will need to start the process by completing a simple gap analysis. Consider where the employee is transferring from, and what the key differences are between that job and the one they will move into. Once you have established the gap, you can begin to consider how you might address that gap. You might consider some of the following approaches:

1 *Connecting the new role/team goal/functional objectives to the overall company strategy*
   In the same way as the 'making connections' tool (Section 14) demonstrates for a large group of employees, your transferee needs to be able to connect what they do now with the team, and to understand how what they do supports the delivery of the overall business strategy or goal. Ask them to work through this process as a starting point (a template

Table 8.1 Connections template

Company goal	Contribution	Functional initiatives	Team initiatives	How I can contribute
Lift the company goals directly as written from where they are published.	Consider whether the team/function has a direct contribution (ie will specifically contribute to the delivery of the goal) or whether their involvement is more indirect.	List any functional initiatives that might contribute to this goal – and how.	List any team initiatives that might contribute to this goal – and how.	Identify ways in which you think your role can contribute to this goal. Identify the functional/team initiatives that you can contribute to.

is shown in Table 8.1 for individuals to self-assess and you to review), but ongoing discussion and dialogue may be required to support their understanding.

2 *Stakeholder matrix – who are the key stakeholders for the work in this new role and what degree of influence do they have over our individual and team success?*

It will be beneficial to the transferee to understand who the key stakeholders are for this new role /team. Ask them to complete a stakeholder matrix (a sample stakeholder matrix template is shown in Figure 8.1) by discussing with their colleagues. This will help to build their knowledge, but also their relationships within the new team. Ask the transferee to note the internal and external stakeholders on the appropriate point on the influence scale. Stakeholders could be individuals, teams, functions, customer segments, etc.

Figure 8.1 Stakeholder matrix template

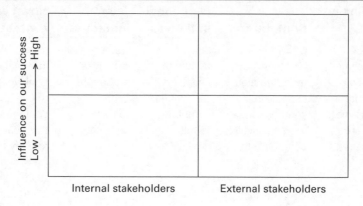

3 *Committing to the job*

Ask the employee to complete a commitment card (see Section 1) to help them to express what they see as the important parts of the role.

Hints and tips

- Involve the transferring employee in the design and the planning of the re-engagement plan. Asking for their view of the differences between past and future roles may help them to appreciate some of the gaps and changes to be addressed. You could ask them to complete a from/to analysis – or add some creativity by asking them to think about it through the 'analogies' tool (see Section 2).

- Preparing the existing team for the arrival of the new starter will be beneficial to ensuring that they know who to expect, and what experience they will bring with them.

Evaluation

Initially, it is useful to understand the value that the transferring employee has found in the activities that you provided for them. Ask them to share their feedback with you.

It is most interesting to evaluate the effectiveness it has had on the transferring employee's work, and their connections to the team.

39 Re-enable

Re-enabling the employee at the point of their transfer from one department, function or internal company is important to ensure that they have the information, skills, equipment and responsibilities, and that they understand the related processes and decision-making authorities within the new role. Whilst a standard induction plan may cover some of these elements, there are factors that may not traditionally be included, and this tool seeks to propose alternative ways to address those.

Best for

Re-enablement is targeted at employees who are transferring from one role to another. Whether that transfer requires them to change function, business unit, geography, etc will only influence how much re-enablement is required.

Best when

Re-enablement is critical to allow the employee to have an effective start in their new job, so planning these things in advance will be important. Delays to simple issues such as IT equipment or passwords can be frustrating, so be proactive in your planning.

Resources

The re-enablement activities will take time to plan, and time from yourself and other key stakeholders to implement, but are unlikely to incur any direct cost.

Outcomes

The goal for re-enablement is that transferred employees are quickly able to start doing their new job, feel able to add value and contribute to team performance. This will help the employee to feel more engaged with the team, and is likely to accelerate their settlement into the new role.

Process

1 Revisit the enablement tool (see Section 5) and determine which of the actions you need to take for your transferee.

2 Complete the template – or your own adaptation of it – for your transferee.

3 Implement the enablement plan.

4 Review with the transferee on a weekly basis during their first three months to ensure progress is being made.

Hints and tips

Be proactive – aim to have everything ready on their first day in their new office.

Evaluation

It is useful to understand how efficient your planning has been in enabling the transferring employee to get started in their new role. Ask them to share their feedback with you, and focus on things that went well, and things that you could improve for future new starters.

On retirement 09

40 Mentoring

Mentoring is defined as 'off-line help by one person to another in making significant transitions in knowledge, work or thinking' (Clutterbuck and Megginson, 1999). This is a great initiative for the retiree as it provides an opportunity to transfer not just traditional knowledge, but also broader experiences, legacy and wisdom from a lifetime's work to a younger or more junior member of staff. Developing the skills of the mentor demonstrates an ongoing value in the retiree, rather than just encouraging them to 'wind down', and can help to ensure that the risks of losing the retiree's knowledge and experience are proactively minimized. As well as the benefits to the retiree and to the business, there is also great benefit to the mentee, who is able to learn from the experiences of their mentor through this process.

Best when

Mentoring can be appropriate at any time, and is not just for the retiree. However, this tool is designed around maintaining high levels of engagement with retirees, hence the focus. This is best introduced at least 12 months prior to the retirement taking place, which provides sufficient time for the retiree to be trained as a mentor, and to see through a period of time as a mentor to one or many mentees.

Best for

In this tool, the focus is on adopting pending retirees as mentors in your organization. Whilst there are certain qualities and characteristics that make a great mentor, there are no limitations on functional speciality, seniority or longevity of service. This suggests, therefore, that you can consider any of your pending retirees for mentor roles within the organization, provided they attend some training and demonstrate the appropriate characteristics to make it a success.

Regardless of the size of your organization, retiring mentors can work effectively – in smaller organizations you will have a smaller pool of potential mentees – but don't lose the opportunity by assuming it won't work.

Resources

You may want to invest in some formal training for your proposed mentors, or you may be able to run a short introductory session in-house. As a priority you need to ensure that proposed mentors understand the process, the expectations and some of the core skills required to make mentoring effective (questioning, listening, feedback, objective setting, etc).

It can also be extremely useful to mirror that training for the mentees, so that both parties are aligned as to the process and expectations of mentoring in your organization.

A nominated individual might be useful to co-ordinate the mentoring scheme, but this could be part of a training or HR co-ordinator's role.

Outcomes

Adopting your pending retirees as potential mentors is intended to support more junior or less experienced employees by providing mentoring to add to their development. The transfer of knowledge, skills and legacy experience will help to ensure that important elements are not lost as the retiree leaves the organization. And of course it is intended that the simple act of nominating, training and utilizing a pending retiree as a mentor will help to retain their commitment and engagement to the organization as they begin to wind down from full-time working. Providing them with new skills and experiences towards the end of their career with you may offer them further opportunities (either employed or in the voluntary sector) during their retirement.

Process

1 Prepare a list of those employees due to retire in the coming 12-month period. From that list identify those who might make good mentors for more junior employees. Consider the strengths and experiences they have and how those could be utilized through mentoring.

2 Identify employees who may benefit from a retiree mentor. Consider what their learning or development needs are, and what personality type or preferences they might have.

3 Match mentors to mentees. There are a number of ways to do this, which include a top-down selection, based on your knowledge of both parties; or, in larger organizations, you may consider a matching event that facilitates the meeting of numerous mentors and mentees, leading to self-selection between them (co-ordinated centrally to ensure a spread of workload).

4 Allow the mentoring relationship to begin, with the setting of some learning objectives as the starting point of the process. How the process works logistically (timing, location, duration, etc) should be left to the two parties to manage themselves.

5 Ending the relationship is an important part of the process. Marking the close of the mentoring process will ensure that both parties can formally review the intended outcomes or objectives, and can consider from both sides the successes and lessons learnt from the experience. Simply allowing the process to drift may impact its credibility, and can leave participants feeling unfulfilled. Mark the ending and celebrate the successes.

Hints and tips

Depending on your approach, this is not an initiative that needs a company-wide communication. There is no harm in keeping it low key, and indeed some mentors and mentees may feel more comfortable with that approach.

Evaluation

Inviting feedback from both the mentor and the mentee will provide high-level feedback on how they felt about the process. For a deeper level of evaluation, consider whether the mentee (and maybe the mentor too) has achieved the development goals they set for themselves.

41 Celebrating career

As employees reach retirement, or leave your organization after a long career, it can be pleasing for both parties to give consideration to the career path the employee has taken, celebrate their successes and recognize the challenges they have overcome. The career celebration allows time for thinking about what progress has been made, what lessons have been learnt and the employee's own thoughts about where the business or its people can go next.

Best when

The career celebration is best utilized in the months prior to an employee planning to leave your organization – and with retirees, this should be easy to arrange as their retirement should not come as an unexpected surprise. However, timing is critical – if you leave it too late, you may not get all the benefits of the process in relation to handover and knowledge transfer; but if you do it too early, the retiree may not feel ready to hand over, or to celebrate their career 'ending'. Ideally, you will run this session in the two to three months prior to the employee's retirement or leave date.

Best for

This is a great tool to use when an employee has long service with you – but not exclusively. It is ideally positioned for retirees, as it allows you to think about and plan the knowledge transfer – sharing their experiences, skills and information with other members of your team. You might also consider the legacy knowledge – the things that you think are unimportant or historical but might one day be incredibly useful. It could be equally valuable for an employee who has been with you for a few years.

Resources

The career celebration is a no-cost activity – apart from the time taken to engage with the retiree, and a venue, all you need are pens and paper.

Outcomes

By considering someone's career timeline, the organization can begin to prepare for their transition away from the company. You can begin to understand what knowledge you may need to transfer to other employees, and start to consider succession planning if you haven't already. As the line manager you can gain a better understanding of what support the employee might need from you in the move towards retirement.

It is engaging because it demonstrates an interest in their career history and achievements, and through discussion the employee may be encouraged to contribute to the organization's future. You can ask them what they think is great about the company, but also what could be changed and their input to future direction. You can take their views about the training and development needed to be able to do their role. You can ask them about their willingness to mentor, coach or train junior staff or colleagues. It enables a continued commitment and engagement with the employee as they head towards retirement.

Process

1 Explain the objective of the process.

2 Along the bottom of a piece of paper draw a horizontal axis and mark the timeline you want to consider (eg full career, only the time with your business etc) in meaningful periods of time. Draw a vertical axis representing level of satisfaction, from low to high.

3 Draw a line parallel to the timeline in the middle of the sheet that identifies a 'reasonable' level of satisfaction.

4 Start by asking the employee to put an X at the appropriate points to indicate change of job/company, placing it so that the level of work-based satisfaction is apparent.

5 Using those milestones as a guide, encourage the employee to think about the achievements, successes and other key milestones in their career and join up the Xs to show the career timeline.

6 Keep challenging to make sure you have a broad range of stories – note some of them in the boxes provided in order to begin to create the stories, the lessons learnt, the top tips and the knowledge management priorities.

7 Join up the Xs to show the career timeline.

Hints and tips

You might find it useful to provide a pre-prepared template and ask the employee to lightly prepare for the session – some will find that reflection time useful, others will be happy to brainstorm it with you.

Evaluation

- What has the process taught you about the employee, their role and how you will manage after their exit that you didn't already know?
- How does this help to prepare you for handover?
- How does the employee feel at the end of the process?

On leaving   10

Farewell letter

When someone leaves the organization you might typically get a card signed, maybe even give a leaving speech. Have you ever thought about writing a letter as well? It is a highly personalized approach to recognition – a letter to an individual leaving your organization to thank them for their service. By highlighting their value, you maintain a level of engagement with the employee despite their leaving – and that may be important in future employment, considering their likelihood of rerun, or maybe just for your employer brand and reputation. It is a good story to hear – that the final note was a positive letter from a former boss, and it is a keepsake that might be valued.

Best for

The farewell letter is appropriate for employees who are leaving the organization and are considered to be 'regrettable' losses – ie those employees you would want to stay. Typically this would mean strong or good performers, those with specialist knowledge, or those with long service who take away a great deal of company knowledge as they leave. It is most likely to be employees who have resigned, but this might also be appropriate for those leaving as part of a voluntary redundancy programme, and retirees.

Best when

The farewell letter is best sent at the time the employee leaves, rather than during their notice period. You should not delay it until after they have left, as it may lose impact.

Resources

There are no direct resource requirements, but writing a letter will take some time to prepare.

Outcomes

Maintaining the engagement of a leaver is a worthwhile activity. First, it provides a positive ending to an employee's relationship with the company, and they are therefore more likely to maintain a positive memory of the organization. Employer reputation will be important as the employee leaves and tells stories of their time in your employment. Maintaining a strong employer brand is important in the recruitment marketplace and for retaining your existing staff.

Process

1 When an employee resigns, you should take this as the trigger point to start preparing your farewell letter.

2 Prepare the letter. Focus on making this a personal note, which takes the opportunity to reflect on the things that have gone well. Provide some positive feedback that reminds the individual of a situation they were involved in, the action they took and the impact that it had. Handwrite the letter if you can.

3 Consider getting some inputs from others for material for your letter – be it colleagues or your own peers. Include stories that support your own messages in the letter.

4 Issue the letter to the employee. You might want to do that in person, in private, during their final days at work, or you might take a view that they would value it more if it arrived at their home address through the post in the days after they have left. Personalize the delivery approach based on what you know about the employee and how they might prefer to receive it.

Hints and tips

Many company policies will prevent you writing a detailed reference for an employee, and will limit such requests to a simple confirmation of employment dates and job titles. The farewell letter is not intended as a reference in any way, but is simply a personal note between yourself and the employee, and as such you might want to mark it that way (eg as 'addressee only', or 'private and confidential'). If in doubt, check with your HR team.

Evaluation

Has any feedback been received as a result of your letter – either directly from the leaver or from other colleagues who had been made aware of it?

For business improvement   11

43 Idea hub

The idea hub is a dedicated space in your office where employees can 'play' to inspire and evoke their own creativity and innovation. The space is designed to be markedly different to the normal working environment, encouraging different thinking, offering freedom from constraints of the 'normal' work-space and inspiring people to think differently. Using different tools and techniques to stimulate the senses aims to ignite some creativity.

Best Companies research in 2015 found that most people want to work in an inspiring environment that offers them some freedom to experiment and try things out. They suggest that providing employees with the oppor-tunity to demonstrate their creativity can make them feel good, can deliver tangible business results and can increase engagement levels.

> 'Innovation happens when people are given the freedom to ask questions and the resources and power to find the answers.'
>
> *Richard Branson*

Best when

The idea hub is useful if you are keen to encourage creativity, innovation, new thinking and redesign. If you want fresh and unusual ideas to stimulate product development, innovative service design, process reinvention, etc, then providing a dedicated space to enable it to happen will be beneficial.

Best for

The idea hub will work well in any organization that welcomes – and has opportunity and appetite to act upon – new ideas and new thinking. All employees can be encouraged to spend time in the hub.

Resources

You will need to allocate some office space to create the idea hub, and to ensure it is seen as a real and valuable investment by the leadership of the organization it should be a meaningful space not just a spare corner. However, that does not mean it has to be huge. You can judge the space you need based on the number of employees you have, how big the teams are and how much 'creative kit' you want to install.

You will need to invest in the 'creative kit' and decor that inspire participants. These will need to be reviewed, refreshed and re-engineered frequently – a stale environment might only inspire stale thinking, so your budget requirement is more than a one-off set-up cost.

That said, you don't need to invest heavily. Most of the items on the creative kit wish list (see 'Hints and tips', below) are not expensive, but making sure they are readily available and in good working order will be important to maintain participants' interest and enthusiasm.

Outcomes

The idea hub is intended to provide your teams and/or individuals with a creative space where they can consider the next stages of evolution – or revolution – for your business. The outcomes should be a stream of ideas and suggestions about how to do things differently or better, some of which will be viable, some of which may not. It is important, though, to recognize the value of the learning and experimentation process as much as it is to consider the tangible and implemented outcomes.

Process

1 Allocate a person responsible for the idea hub initiative – enlisting a senior sponsor in the organization will give the initiative some weight and encourage greater support from all levels in the organization. Set a budget that enables the hub to be set up and maintained.

2 Set up your idea hub. Allocate the space and provide the appropriate 'creative kit' for your business, your space and your preferred outcomes.

3 Communicate the purpose and goals of the idea hub. Be clear on the expectations about how it should be used.

4 Enable and encourage participation. Role modelling will help, but your managers need to make it acceptable for people to spend time in the hub just 'exploring'.

5 Pose business challenges for hub participants – if there is a specific business challenge or opportunity that you need ideas about then make that clear. You may even want to set up a specific 'hit squad' to work it through.

6 Acting upon ideas will be important – if nothing happens when ideas or suggestions are put forward, then people will stop participating. Make sure that the process is clear – when someone has an idea, how do they get that to the key decision makers? Make sure people know and understand the route – but don't make it too bureaucratic so that people are put off by barriers in their way. Keep the process agile and responsive.

7 Share successes when they happen. If ideas are followed up and implemented, communicate that across the business. If they are unsuccessful, talk openly about why, and focus on the learning that has been gained from the experience and the process.

Hints and tips

- Have some time when there is a trained facilitator present – it might be just an hour or it could be a full day. By using an internal or external facilitator in the hub, you may be able to bring teams together to focus on a challenge but in a more focused way.

- Use the idea hub – instead of a standard meeting room – as an alternative space for your team briefings, meetings or stand-ups.

- Continuous development of the space is important – there is an irony in not refreshing or reinventing a space designed specifically for the purpose of reinvention itself!!

- Suggested 'creative kit' contents:

Stimulating the senses – seeing
- books on creativity, innovation, design, architecture;
- mindfulness colouring books;
- supplies of coloured marker pens, felt tips, wax crayons;
- flipcharts, whiteboards, large sketch pads;
- an internet screen connected to TED Talks or YouTube;
- Lego/building blocks;
- Post-it notes in different shapes, colours, sizes;
- coloured paper and card in different shapes, sizes, textures, etc;

- large boards for mood boards;
- foam shapes;
- stickers;
- large blank spaces (walls, glass whiteboards, windows);
- graffiti walls;
- furniture: not the normal furnishings, instead go for unusual designs, bright colours, strange shapes, relaxing not formal such as beanbags, coffee tables, rocking chairs, bar stools, high bar tables, bistro sets, etc.

Stimulating the senses – hearing

- music, iPod, radio, video;
- ambient sounds: nature, waves, birdsong, etc;
- water feature.

Stimulating the senses – feeling

- sensory toys: balls, blocks, texture tangles, stress balls, bendy man, twist and lock blocks (look for 'fiddle kits' online).

Stimulating the senses – tasting

- provide drinks, food, snacks.

Stimulating the senses – smelling

- plants and flowers;
- scents, coffee.

About your business

- your product: old and new versions, toy versions, extreme versions, all variations;
- pictures/imagery of your typical customer;
- flowcharts of process;
- high-level business operating model flow.

Other inspiration

- business model navigator cards.
- If you are not really interested in novel ideas or approaches then this is not for you – and not only will you waste money but you are likely to

disengage your teams. You need to ensure that employees and teams are encouraged to visit the space, and that any outcomes from their time there are fully considered by the appropriate parties, that feedback is provided, and that successful outcomes or great learnings are shared and celebrated.

Evaluation

There are a number of ways that you can measure the effectiveness of the idea hub, depending on what matters most to you and your business.

Hard measures will demonstrate the return on your investment, so you could consider what ideas have been implemented, how much money has been saved, the degree to which efficiency or service have been improved (eg days in supply chain, service satisfaction rating, work in progress, stock value, etc).

Softer measures might focus on the utility of the hub – how many employees are making use of it, how long they are spending in the hub, and the level of storytelling about the hub experience.

In the middle, you may look for metrics about the number of ideas generated or suggestions put forward, and consider qualitative measures around lessons learnt, indirect benefits, team building and collaboration, and overall levels of engagement.

44   Connecting lessons

Connecting lessons is a process to bring together teams of people to help each other to solve problems or generate ideas based on their own previous experiences of similar challenges. It encourages the sharing of expertise, but perhaps more importantly, the sharing of lessons learnt, things that have worked and things that haven't, with some explanation and clarification as to why. This latter part of the process is important, as some things may not have worked in previous scenarios but, with adaptations or a different context, could be very effective.

The connecting lessons process brings together people from across the organization, and can almost act as a peer training event, though it is not formally set up as such. The 'connecting' in the title of this activity refers to two different opportunities to connect – the first is the connections between earlier lessons learnt and future activities of a similar or relatable nature. The second is the connections between project teams or teams of experts, who in larger organizations may not otherwise have cause to meet or to work together.

It engages teams in both successful delivery of their projects and in collaborating with others in the organization.

> 'Learn from yesterday, live for today, hope for tomorrow. The important thing is not to stop questioning.'
>
> *Albert Einstein*

Best when

Connecting lessons is most effective when there is a clear problem or challenge to be addressed. If the purpose is less specific then an alternative tool is more likely to work. For connecting lessons to be effective, there needs to be clarity of purpose and a challenge that the group can work on together. It is most effective when facilitated by an independent party from the groups (ie a manager or trainer from another department or function) to ensure that the process is followed and the purpose is achieved.

This is an ideal activity to support a formally structured project, or a project kick-off activity. For example, if you were to implement a new system, regardless of its technical spec, it could be interesting to hear from the team who recently implemented something similar in a different part of the organization.

Best for

The nature of connecting lessons suggests that it is particularly useful in larger organizations, where projects may be replicated or similar initiatives followed across different functions, geographies or legal entities. Whilst this may be true there may be some elements of connecting lessons that could transfer into smaller organizations.

This tool will work effectively with all levels and functions in the organization. However, you will need to ensure that the participants all have an understanding of the challenge or previous experience of a similar (or the same) challenge.

Resources

Connecting lessons is primarily a discussion group, and therefore does not require any major resource requirements. You will need to allocate a meeting space, and the time for all participants to attend and commit to the process. A facilitator will be needed to ensure that the process remains on track and that the desired outcomes are achieved. A flipchart and pens will be needed, but try to stay away from PowerPoint presentations and focus on discussion instead.

Outcomes

Connecting lessons can have a range of positive outcomes for the teams involved, for the success of the project, and for the organization as a whole. The team offering their experience get to share their experiences and lessons learnt, and to influence how future projects or similar activities may be adapted based on their own previous experience. This benefits the project, as learnings are applied and similar mistakes can be avoided or opportunities maximized. It means greater likelihood of success and less waste (of time, of money, of resources), which benefits the company's bottom line, product quality, service efficiency or customer experience.

Process

1 Identify an opportunity for a connecting lessons session. You will most likely have identified a project or an initiative that would make good subject matter, and so agreeing the nature of the challenge with the team involved, and what help they might find useful, will be an important first step. Ideally from this project team you would identify around six participants who will cover a breadth of specialisms or functions within the project (eg the technical expert, the project manager, the people person, the trainer, etc).

2 Clarify with the team the scope that they need help with. This could range from a specific challenge (eg how do we communicate with our international customers about the changes that will happen?) through to the full project life cycle (eg what lessons were learnt at each stage?). The scope may depend on many factors, including what stage the project is at, whether specific challenges have been encountered, etc.

3 Identify an experienced team who can help. They should have had a similar experience, and be able to bring constructive lessons learnt to the process. Matching the team size will be important so that there is a good balance, but it is not necessary to match all the skills or team roles exactly – you might find some benefit in having diversity across the teams.

4 Provide briefings to all participants, and to the facilitator. For the past-experience team, encouraging them to be open and honest about their experiences, and to share both positive and negative experiences, will be important to the success of the session. Encourage the receiving team to be open to new ideas and suggestions, to be inquisitive and challenging, and to interpret their findings and adapt them to solutions that would work best for their project.

5 Set and run the agenda:

   – The facilitator makes introductions, explains the process, the objectives and the desired outcome.

   – The receiving team outlines the scope – the challenge they face, or an overview of the project – and what they want to achieve through the connecting lessons session.

   – The experienced team begin their session by asking questions and encouraging further discussion to ensure that they fully understand the issue. This can be done in a full group discussion around the table, or you can encourage a more informal 'speed dating' style of conversation – each participant wandering the room to talk to individuals one-to-one. A mix of these two approaches will work well.

   – Back around the table the experienced team will play back what they understand to be the challenge or scope to be discussed.

   – The two teams will then separate for a period of time. It is useful to ask the groups how long they need, but be aware that this could be as much as half a day. The experienced group will discuss what challenges or issues they have gathered from the receiving team, and what lessons or experiences they have had that are relevant or transferrable. They should be prepared to tell their own stories from their experiences, and to include what they would do differently in the future.

- Bring the two teams back together and allow the experienced team to present back to the receiving team their ideas, suggestions and recommendations. Encourage them to support each key point with their own experiences – the learning will be stronger if the receiving team can relate to or understand the issues that led to the lessons learnt.

- Allow the receiving team the opportunity to challenge and raise questions to the experienced team in order to ensure that they fully understand what is being discussed and proposed. Allow the receiving team to take some time out to consider what has been discussed, and to prepare their final comments.

- As a closing statement, the receiving team present back their next steps and actions in the light of the outcomes of the connecting lessons.

6 In closing the session the facilitator should reflect back on the objectives and outcomes of the session to ensure that they have been fulfilled.

Hints and tips

- If the teams don't know each other at the start of the process, a fun ice-breaker at the start of the session may encourage a more informal style of workshop.

- Encourage participants to consider who else might benefit from connected lessons, and to be advocates for the process.

- Consider involving a third team – the independent team. This team could be similar in number (or smaller) but would have no prior knowledge or experience of the given project, or similar initiatives. The advantage they could bring to the process would be their fresh perspectives – with no prior knowledge, they might be able to offer up ideas and suggestions that neither team had considered to date. Of course this would add time to the process, to allow them to gain understanding (in parallel with the experienced team) and to consider their own recommendations. However, for some additional quality content it may be worthwhile.

- Create a community of connected lessons specialist facilitators – a small group of people who can become experts in the process, and use it across your organization.

Evaluation

A quick 'happy sheet' or end-of-session brainstorm will allow you to identify quickly whether participants enjoyed and valued the process, and what they feel might be done differently to continually improve upon it. (An example 'happy sheet' is provided in Table 16.2 at the end of this book.)

However, the value in connecting lessons is the impact it has on future projects, and so the focus of evaluation should be on measuring whether the process has had any real impact on how things are done within future projects.

At the broadest level of evaluation, ask the receiving team how many of the recommendations were actually implemented – this gives an indication of how much impact the session had on them, and provides some insight into the credibility they perceived in those recommendations.

At a deeper level of evaluation, you will need to understand the impact of that implementation – did it have the desired effect? Of course it is difficult to compare what was done to what might have been done, because there is no evidence. However, you can check that none of the risks described by the experienced team were repeated after the connecting lessons session.

In change   12

Change champions

The change champions are a support network that you can create during times of change, turbulence or uncertainty in your team or business. The champion is intended to be a first port of call for all employees to talk about the changes that are happening. They are strong advocates of an effective change process and of the 'new future' that you are heading towards. They interact with their colleagues about the change and help to secure commitment to it, encouraging the right behaviours for the organization and embedding the change so that it sticks – and is not just seen as 'flavour of the month'.

The CIPD factsheet on change management (CIPD, 2016a) highlights that when change is not implemented effectively it can have a significant impact on the engagement of employees in the organization. Getting employees involved, and giving them a key role in the success of a change initiative, could help to secure engagement through those challenging times.

Best when

Change champions become relevant and important when your organization or team is about to experience some kind of change. It does not have to be major change – you might be changing a system, moving location, taking on a significant new customer or making redundancies. Regardless of the size of your organization, identifying an individual who can really connect with all your employees about the change will be valuable. In larger organizations a team of change champions might be appropriate.

Best for

It is a good idea to make your team of change champions representative of the population they will support. This means you may have champions at a range of levels from various functions if your change impacts the whole organization, or you may only need change champions from a particular grade or level and/or a specific function. However, the selection of change champions is not related to seniority or experience – this role is one that requires the right internal networks, understanding of change, and positive attitudes and behaviours towards change and constructive challenge.

Resources

The change champions are still engaged in their day job – the champion role is an enhancement to that. As such, you may need to account for them spending less time on the job and some time away for training. The cost of training should be considered if it is to be provided externally.

Outcomes

Communication fed informally up and down the organization. You will be able to use the change champions to ensure effective communications – ensuring that key messages and information are getting through all layers of the organization. The champions will be getting feedback – and whilst they should not be expected to report verbatim, or to name individual feedback and comments, they can report on themes, general concerns, opportunities, etc.

Process

1 Understand the change that is being experienced and ensure that you have a clear impact assessment – this will help you to appreciate how it will affect different stakeholder groups.

2 Identify some team members who you consider will react positively to change and who are supporters of the new future. They should be well connected around the organization, open and approachable for a wide range of employees.

3 Train them. Provide training in basic change management skills and tools, but particularly in the change curve and managing people through it. Some basic coaching techniques will also be beneficial.

4 Make them visible. Promote their role and ensure people know who they can chat to about change. Ask them to attend briefings and workshops (not just their own) as a support to team managers, and they may even hold 'surgeries' or drop-in sessions for employees.

5 On a regular basis (depending on the project timeline) ask them to provide themes and feedback to you and your management team. They will need to be tuned in to what is happening in the organization, the informal

feedback and back-room discussions, and they must have the confidence to be able to speak up about those themes to the senior managers in the business. This will help you to structure your communication and may provide you with ideas and insights for the change that you had not considered.

6 Whenever you take something like this into account, feed it back down the line through your champions – it demonstrates that the process is working and allocates credit where it is due.

7 When the change is completed and the project closes, celebrate the success of your change champions group – buy them a bottle of wine or a box of chocolates, for example.

Hints and tips

- You could consider providing 'Change Champion' T-shirts for the designated change champions. During busy times, it may be beneficial to spotlight who they are and make them very accessible to their colleagues.

- Recognizing the efforts of your change champions will be important at the end of the change programme, thanking them for their commitment and recognizing that they have had a key role in the successful implementation of a change. It may be a letter, a bottle of wine or cinema tickets, etc – it doesn't have to be costly, but the gesture will no doubt be appreciated.

Evaluation

You should consider a number of factors in evaluating the effectiveness of the change champion.

You could consider the performance of the individual change champions themselves – have they remained as advocates, talking positively about change, and providing great responses and support to individuals when challenged?

You might also take a view of the feedback received and channelled back up the line. Has the provision of change champions enabled that feedback to flow more freely? Note the themes of the feedback and how they have helped to shape the change programme or process.

Finally, consider the overall implementation of the change, the degree of commitment from employees, and the time taken to move from transition to realizing benefits. You may be able to connect the role played by change champions to the depth of buy-in and the speed execution of new ways of working.

46   Preparing for change

> 'The only thing that is constant is change.'
>
> *Heraclitus*

Change is happening all the time. In your business, you may gain new customers, lose old customers, you may have to cut costs or you may have a significant investment. You may choose to develop new ways of working, change the ways you service customers or introduce new machinery or technology to your process. These are all great examples of everyday change. You will constantly be changing the ways in which you work in order to stay relevant, excellent and in business. Proactively helping your employees to manage change will encourage them to be more resilient, a stronger advocate for your change, and more engaged in the change process itself.

Research suggests that some of the main contributors to the failure of change programmes is that the managers are unprepared and unskilled in leading change, and communication is poor. Employees do not understand the rationale for the change and what role they should play. By running a preparatory workshop you can prepare, share and involve.

People don't like having change done to them. They feel a loss of control as decisions are made without their input or their expertise. By proactively involving them in preparing themselves for change, and maybe being part of it, that loss of control could be minimized as they participate more willingly.

Best when

Ideally you would encourage your employees to be ready for change proactively, as part of your ongoing development programme. If this is not realistic in your business, providing people with some support at the point of change can still be extremely valuable.

Best for

Change affects everyone, but it is important to recognize that it will affect everyone in different ways, and in different timelines. Some people will learn of change, adapt to it and start new ways of working all in a matter of moments. Others will take significantly longer. This depends on many factors, but is typically driven by individual personality rather than function, seniority or education. It is appropriate to engage with your leaders and managers first, as they will need to take on the task of supporting their team members through the change process. However, you should not expect that they will automatically commit to the change – they may take some time too. Preparing all staff for change, however, will be critical to the success of any change that you want to implement.

The nature of the change is immaterial. Whilst the level of disruption or the degree of change may vary (eg from introducing a new piece of machinery to a fundamental reorganization of how you work) there should be some consideration of the change support that your teams may need. It could be a small-scale consideration, but a conscious choice to consider it – rather than just 'get on and implement' – will ensure that you take account of your employees' needs.

Resources

You might want to consider investing in a specialist trainer or facilitator to run a workshop for you. However, if you do, make sure the content is relevant to your organizational culture, the change you are going through and the dynamics of your business.

If you choose to facilitate internally, you will need to allocate time to prepare the materials and content for the workshop, as well as consider the time required for people to attend.

Outcomes

At the end of a 'preparing for change' workshop participants would be more aware of the process of change: ie how you intend to make change happen in your business. The workshop should encourage discussion, debate, feedback and commitment.

Participants would have a better understanding of how people in general respond to change, and should have been given time to reflect on what that means for them. This self-reflection in turn allows them to consider what they may need from their manager or colleagues, but also what they have to offer through the process of change.

If you are describing a specific change initiative, the 'preparing for change' workshop encourages understanding, buy-in and commitment to your new direction.

Process

1 Explaining the rationale for change. Describing the 'what' and 'why' of change is important and should not be overlooked. In order to make a transition, employees may need to understand what is not working 'now' and how and why things need to be different.

2 Describing the vision and the 'from/to'. Explaining to people in your own words what the future looks like will help them to envisage it, and to consider what they need to do to make things different.

3 Explaining what will happen next and how/when the change will be implemented is important. Employees will want to understand what the immediate next steps are, what they have to do and who has what role in the change.

4 Explain how people might react. Different people will react in different ways, and it is important for you to recognize that, but also for colleagues to recognize it in each other. It will allow them opportunity to support each other, and to empathize throughout the change process.

5 Explain how they can get involved. For those who want to actively participate in shaping or implementing the future vision, you should find ways to engage them – through focus groups, to act as advocates or sponsors, or to contribute ideas, comments and feedback.

Hints and tips

- A number of the tools described in this book will be relevant and helpful to you in setting up this process, particularly 'dialogue sheets', 'making connections', 'idea wall' and 'analogies' tools.

- Research some change management models but keep it really simple – blinding people with science and management theory is not the goal. Find practical and useful approaches that feel relevant to your company culture and your business and that your employees are likely to identify with.

- A few simple recommended approaches are listed below, and you can find out more information about each of them on the internet:
  - the change curve;
  - bridges transitions;
  - ADKAR.

A simple change readiness assessment is shown in Table 12.1.

Table 12.1 Change readiness assessment

Change Aspect	Enablers	Readiness	Comments/Actions
Vision	The vision for new ways of working is clearly articulated in simple terms. The vision has been shared with all employees.	☺ ☺ ☹	
Leadership	Senior managers in the business are engaged in the change, and are able to lead their teams through it.	☺ ☺ ☹	
Rationale	The reason for the change is clear and has been explained to all employees in simple terms. It is clear what was not satisfactory. Benefits of the change are understood.	☺ ☺ ☹	
Capacity	The organization has the capacity to allocate resources to the change, and to support employees through the change process.	☺ ☺ ☹	
Communication	A communication plan is in place to share information and progress about the change on an ongoing basis.	☺ ☺ ☹	
History	Previous experiences of change in this organization have been positive and inclusive.	☺ ☺ ☹	
Temperature check	The mood of the organization is optimistic. People are excited about the future.	☺ ☺ ☹	

Evaluation

Completion of a 'happy sheet' at the end of the workshop will confirm if participants have enjoyed the workshop and whether it has met its objectives. (An example is provided in Table 16.2 at the end of this book.)

However, the real value in the workshop is that your organization should feel better prepared and enabled for change. A change readiness assessment will guide you as to how effective the workshop has been in preparing your employees.

For customer focus

13

Shadowing the customer

Customer shadowing encourages an employee to spend the day with one of your customers, experiencing the work your customer does, and particularly that part of their work that relates to your business – from your customer's perspective.

It proposes that one or two of your employees work in the customer's offices, shadowing some of their key departments and learning about how they operate. By connecting with the customer in this way you can understand better where you fit in to their overall service proposition, and you may learn a few things about how you can improve what you do for them, how you can help them and maybe even how you can sell more or upsell to them.

By involving employees in this way, they can become involved in making improvements and changes. As a bottom-up approach, it is likely to be more engaging to employees, and they are more likely to support implementation and the commitment to it.

Best when

This approach is best implemented when you have a confident and well established or long-standing relationship with the customer. You will need to ensure that your customer is comfortable with this initiative, and is able to brief participating employees on their side. The relationship needs to be strong so that your employee can confidently spend time with the customer, and for the duration of their experience is able to focus on opportunities to make things even better, rather than having to focus on addressing complaints and concerns.

Best for

Ideally an employee whose work has an impact – direct or indirect – on the customer would be selected for this initiative, but regardless of seniority or function within the business. Bear in mind that this employee will be a showcase for your organization, so you should identify a participant who can act as a strong advocate for your business, and who can take some ownership of any opportunities identified. However, do not read this as needing to be a manager – this could still be an employee at any level.

An alternative approach is to identify an employee to participate who works with the product or the customer and who would not typically have regular interaction with them.

Resources

You will need to allocate a day for the visit to take place, and should build this into your resource planning. It is likely that you will need to allocate a small budget to cover minor expenses.

If your goal is to encourage improvement recommendations, you might need to set aside a budget to fund these initiatives. If financial constraints are likely to limit that, be clear about it in your briefings and encourage participants to focus only on no-cost or low-cost initiatives.

Outcomes

Your employees should have a better understanding of the customer – and more empathy with them should problems arise. Employees will feel that you listened to them and they had a voice, and you should see some customer-facing improvements – including service, quality- and/or efficiency-focused recommendations as a result of the visit.

Process

1 Establish the customer's willingness to participate. Explain the rationale for the initiative and what you hope to get out of it, with a particular focus on the connection to the customer.

2 Agree a date and time for the visit, confirming the contact details and travel arrangements required.

3 Brief your selected visitors on the purpose of the exercise, and your expectations of them on their return.

4 On returning, arrange an immediate debrief with the participants to gain their initial and informal insights.

5 Once they have had time to reflect on their own experiences during the visit, encourage a more formal presentation of recommendations.

Hints and tips

- Ask the employee(s) who took part in the visit to share their insights from the day with others who might benefit. This could be through a chew and chat session (see Section 6) or during a stand-up (see Section 2).

- There may need to be some areas where you explicitly restrict disclosure. You may not want your employees discussing their awareness of cost structures, pricing, supplier relations, etc, for commercial reasons. If this is the case, be explicit in the brief about what should not be discussed and why.

- Run this as an exchange programme – you send to the customer, they send someone to you.

Evaluation

You can evaluate the level of interest in this initiative by assessing how many nominations or volunteers you received for participation. However, the key goal of the shadowing experience is to gain a better understanding of the customer, so assessing how effective it has been in that light will be most important. Consider:

- What did you learn about the customer as a result of the shadowing experience?

- How will that impact on your service delivery, etc?

- What opportunities does that present to your business offerings to that – and any other – customer?

- Ultimately, has this had a positive effect on your financial position:

  - Are sales increasing?
  - Have you been able to up-sell or cross-sell?
  - Have there been less returns, product quality issues raised, etc?

And

  - Are customer service reviews up?
  - Are relationships between the two parties improving?

48　The customer experience

This initiative empowers your team members to experience being a customer for a day and get a sense of your service, quality, pricing or value by seeing it from the customer's perspective.

Part of the experience may be competitor comparisons too – comparing products, quality, pricing, service – and generally shopping around, which your customer might do, to get alternatives and to understand how your offering matches up. Consider combining the customer experience with the benchmarking roadtrip (see Section 1).

Best when

The customer experience initiative will be most effective when your business is stable and performing well – you can look for 'even better' opportunities. It will be less effective if you already have improvement plans in place – adding to a list of outstanding actions will not be of benefit. However, you may use it to check how your improvements are impacting customer experience.

Ideally, your employees will be able to role-play the customer experience – eg as a customer in your store or dialling in to your customer service centre, or simply using one of the products or services you deliver.

Best for

This initiative is best suited to employees who deal with the product or the customer and who would not typically have regular interaction with them.

Resources

You will need to allocate a day for the visit to take place, as well as some budget for any expenses incurred (ie if the product or service needs to be bought, if there is travel involved, etc).

You also might need to consider some investment for any improvement initiatives that are identified through the course of the customer experience. Doing nothing with the recommendations that are presented to you will disengage those employees involved, and whilst cost may not always be required it is beneficial to have guidance on that at the start of the process in order to manage expectations.

Outcomes

Having been put into your customer's shoes for a day, your employees should have a better understanding of them, the challenges they face with your products or services, and subsequently have more empathy with them should problems arise. However, it is not always bad news, and there can also be advantage in having experienced the positives and being able to share those too, both internally, but also in empathy with the pleased customer.

Employees will feel that you listened to them and they had a voice, provided that you respond to their feedback. You may also be able to introduce some customer-facing improvements – taking recommendations from the employee's experience, you may be able to make enhancements to your service, quality, efficiency or cost to the customer.

Process

1 Identify volunteers or handpick your participants. An individual experience can work well depending on your type of organization, but you might consider sending people out in pairs. Two brains might be better than one, and sharing ideas, note taking and discussing experiences together might add value to the outcome.

2 Provide a clear briefing on what you want the participants to do and what a successful day looks like (eg lots of ideas and recommendations – or are you looking for just one thing that will make a difference?).

3 Allow the participants to plan the day as they think appropriate. But if you want to confirm or approve it, be clear that you will review and approve. Be transparent about boundaries and any constraints – eg you may not want them to use video or post anything on social media.

4 Allow them time away from their normal work for this opportunity. Once briefed, they should begin their 'customer' experience.

5 Get an immediate informal review at the end of the day if possible – first thoughts and immediate reactions. If this cannot be done face to face, encourage the participant(s) to send a short bullet-point e-mail with their key takeaways from the experience.

6 Schedule a formal feedback session with what was learnt and any recommendations that have been made.

Hints and tips

Ask the employee(s) who take part in the visit to share their insights from the day with others who might benefit. This could be through a chew and chat session (see Section 6) or during a stand-up (see Section 2).

Evaluation

- What feedback did you get from the employee, and how did this change the way that you work?
- What new initiatives or improvements did you make as a result of the exercise? What impact has that had on your income and finances, on your net promoter score (NPS) or on more general customer feedback, etc?
- Have you had volunteers for this initiative – or are any of your employees coming forward with suggestions or informal feedback?

49   The roadshow

> 'Spend a lot of time talking to customers face to face. You would be amazed how many companies don't listen to their customers.'
>
> *Ross Perot*

The roadshow event follows the format of the internal marketplace (see Section 3) but the focus here is on getting to know customers, suppliers or other external stakeholders. Whilst the principles of the event and its processes are similar there are some important differences, so it has been presented as a separate tool with its own guidance.

The primary difference is the expectations the parties will have of the event and its outcomes, and that there are potentially some greater risks in the roadshow. You should consider how it might affect your reputation or credibility should anything go wrong. However, this shouldn't be your excuse not to do it. It should really only be your stimulus to prepare yourself and your team well and ensure your participants (on all sides) are well briefed.

The roadshow brings your selected stakeholder group (eg customers or suppliers) into one place to promote their company, services, goods, etc and share information about what they do to help to build better relationships with customers and suppliers. This can be advantageous to your business, by enabling your employees to build stronger connections to their key external contacts.

The process asks for each stakeholder to provide an informal display or static presentation – like you might find at a trade show or business fair – and allows your employees the opportunity to walk around and engage, make connections and learn. Enabling them to understand how what they do impacts the customer or supplier's work can have a positive effect on their engagement in their work – they may feel more inclined to provide a quality service or product to those they have interacted with.

Best when

This activity works well when you want to improve your employees' understanding of customers and/or suppliers. Consider whether there is anything happening in your business, or that of your invited guests, that might impact on the event – for example any major news stories, organizational announcements, etc – and that there are no major service or reputational issues between your company and those attending at the time of the event.

Ensuring that attendees from all sides are in a positive place will be important to ensure that good connections are made.

Best for

This is an effective tool for engaging your broad employee population with key customers, suppliers or other important or influential stakeholders (eg professional bodies, regulators, industry groups, etc). However, you will need to be able to demonstrate a value of participating – ie what's in it for them – to those you invite. It is therefore critical that you are able to articulate this early on in the process.

The roadshow will work best if everyone can get involved. Don't leave it to your employees to represent the company – representatives from all levels should attend and participate.

Resources

To be impactful you will need to invest in this process. You should consider the value of really theming the event as a marketplace – organize real market stalls and prepare the presentation and display materials as professionally as you can. Bear in mind that if these are your suppliers they may be willing to bear some cost themselves. However, this should not be a barrier. If the best you can manage is a flipchart with key bullet points about the team, then it will still serve the purpose.

You will need to invest time. This is most effective when everyone downs tools and attends at the same time, so if you are able to, shut down your operation for a couple of hours in order to get the best possible interaction and engagement. Alternatively you can run the roadshow over an extended lunch period, allowing employees the opportunity to explore during their break. Bear in mind, though, that this is likely to be a more voluntary approach. Investing time out of your business – if practical – will be beneficial.

Outcomes

The roadshow is intended to provide a sociable opportunity for your teams and functions to get to know customers, suppliers or other key stakeholders better, to understand more about what they do and how you currently support or motivate them to deliver their own services.

You can develop this outcome to the next level by using the event as an opportunity to identify opportunities to improve those connections or the services that you offer to each other. You can work together to figure out how to create more efficiency between you, by looking at areas where you duplicate work, or where you could reduce administration or improve handover handoff. At the very minimum you begin to build relationships just by putting faces to names.

Process

1 Before your commit to running a roadshow event, take some time to really consider why it is important for you and your business at this time, what you want to achieve through the event, and therefore what or who is important in establishing it.

2 Invite participants. Consider who would be most beneficial to attend, and target those stakeholders first. Be clear in your communication to them about the objectives for the event, what benefits you think they might have in attending, and those for your employees. Be transparent about what is involved, any costs they might incur, and what you want them to bring. If you have done similar events before, some examples or case studies might help them to understand what is proposed.

3 Communicate news of the event and its objectives. Explain what you are planning to do, and why, with a clear indication of why employees will benefit by attending. Keep the communications simple, but provide regular updates on who will be participating, and build momentum in your communications activity up to the day of the event.

4 On the day, have a few employees delegated to run the set-up of the event, ensuring that the participants know where they need to be, what they need to do, and to support any ongoing needs that they have during the day.

5 Run the session. Encourage people to attend by providing prompts on the day, as well as those that you have proactively placed. Your leaders and managers should be strong advocates of the event and should allow people time to attend, and of course should be seen to attend themselves.

6 Send out your thanks. You should thank your stakeholder participants for taking the time to spend the day with your teams, and you should thank your teams for taking some time out to talk to the participants. A reminder to both sets of parties on what was achieved by doing so, and maybe some highlights of the day, will also be beneficial.

7 Evaluate the effectiveness of the session, using some of the suggestions later in this section. Bear in mind that you should evaluate not just the immediate effectiveness of the event (ie did people enjoy attending?) but the longer-term impacts that relate to collaboration, effectiveness of the relationships, the importance of having more knowledge, etc.

Hints and tips

- Encourage participants to make their way around every stall or presentation by offering incentive. If each employee had a 'passport' that they had to get stamped at each stand, there could be a small reward at the end of their journey, for example (a chocolate bar or a coffee!). Or there could be a quiz at the end – and having visited all of the stands they are more likely to perform well.

- Encourage customers or suppliers to bring along products or items that demonstrate more than just their product line. For example, if they operate in a specific location they could bring samples of specialities (food, drinks, specific products or local traditions) from that location (this works particularly well if any of the parties are from or are based overseas).

- Bring demonstrations of their full product line to show the breadth of their service, even if it is out of the scope of your company's remit with them.

- Encourage those displaying to bring branded giveaways for your employees, as well as company literature, documentation and samples.

Evaluation

There are two levels of evaluation for the roadshow. The first is to establish the surface-level effectiveness of the event, and this can be done separately from the perspectives of those displaying and those attending. A simple 'happy sheet' effectiveness questionnaire will work, but you may be asking slightly different questions from each of the two groups. Alternatively for your employees you could check in at the end of your event using the mood board (Section 2), graffiti wall (Section 3) or a similar approach.

A further level of evaluation would consider how much impact the concept and content of the day has had on your employees. For example, are you seeing greater discretionary effort to deliver a good service to customers, suppliers, etc – has the event led them to a greater understanding of how they can be helpful or supportive? Find out if there is more interaction between the parties. You may also notice less formal complaints as issues can be resolved informally between parties who now know and understand each other better, or more compliments about positive experiences. Other than your standard business measurements and metrics, one of the best ways to establish whether any of these effects has been seen is simply to ask people – and if you hear positive stories, share them.

In delivering results

50 Making connections

Making connections is a short but effective strategy cascade process, providing the opportunity to share company strategy and align functional or team goals, sharing information across functions to eliminate silos and encourage greater collaboration. It is run as an informal but structured workshop event, with both functional and cross-functional activities, but can be delivered interactively within just a few hours.

In *A Book About Innocent* (Germain and Reed, 2009) the authors describe the importance that people attach to knowing what is expected of them at work, and emphasize that they ensure there is a clear line of sight between what the company wants to achieve and the individual's objectives. This is heavily supported by the MacLeod Report (MacLeod and Clarke, 2009), commissioned by the UK government, which identified one of four enablers of employee engagement as the 'strategic narrative' – that provides employees with clear connection between what they do in their job and the overall aims of the organization. The report highlights the critical role that leaders and managers can play in helping employees to make that connection, providing both the visibility of it, and the recognition and reward when their part is achieved.

The 'making connections' workshop does just that – it connects an employee's individual work objectives to their overall company goals, and to each other, enabling both alignment and collaboration.

> 'There are only three measurements that tell you nearly everything you need to know about your organization's overall performance: employee engagement, customer satisfaction and cash flow. It goes without saying that no company, small or large, can win over the long run without energized employees who believe in the mission and understand how to achieve it.'
>
> *Jack Welch, former CEO of General Electric*

Best when

The making connections session works well at the time that you have reviewed or reset your business strategy and/or goals, and are ready to share them with your employees. Typically this could be an annual – or maybe bi-annual – process, and it should be aligned to the setting and reviewing of individual performance objectives.

Best for

In larger organizations it can be effective to launch making connections as an all-employee initiative, but implement it by layer as a cascade process. This is primarily for practical reasons of time and space, but the essence is transparency – so if you can get everyone interacting in the same room, all the better. If cascade is the most appropriate for your organization, start with your senior teams, but involve as many layers as is practical in the first session. You should then look to use some of those attendees as advocates, sponsors and facilitators in the next sessions in the cascade.

Resources

Dependent on the number of participants, you may need an external meeting venue (and potential AV support), which is likely to be the bulk of your costs for this event. You will need a room big enough for all your participants to view a presentation and to later move around and talk with each other. More importantly you need a lot of wall space, or display stands to accommodate posters and flipcharts, so make this a high priority when choosing your venue.

Some budget will be required for preparing your materials and purchasing the equipment. A shopping list of materials is provided in the 'Hints and tips' section, below. Posters can be produced relatively cheaply from printing companies (you don't need high-quality paper or print), and if cost is really an issue you can re-create them by hand, using rolls of paper.

The workshop can be run in as little as a few hours. Whether you decide to optimize the time out by adding to that will depend on your objectives for the session and your operational requirements.

Outcomes

By engaging employees in the organization's strategy, they are more likely to feel satisfied at work, engaged in their activities and the company goals, and deliver an improved performance.

By participating in cross-functional workshops, employees will see opportunities for collaboration and synergy – to improve processes and ownership; review ways of working; make things better, cheaper and/or more efficient.

By linking individual objectives to the overall company objectives/measures/targets, we can ensure that all efforts of employees in the organization are working towards the same success – and the same goal.

By clarifying to employees the expectations the company has of them, it is significantly easier to ensure that they meet those expectations. We can do this through aligned objective setting and by ensuring accuracy of job descriptions and day-to-day tasks, and setting performance measures.

Process

Preparation

1 Set the date for the workshop, providing plenty of notice so that people can prioritize it.

2 Book a venue for the appropriate number of people – you may need to find a venue away from your normal place of work, but that is not critical to the effective running of a session. You will need to seat people preferably in a cabaret style but with room for small groups to break out for group discussions.

3 Confirm who will be lead facilitator for the workshop, and depending on the number of attendees you have you might want to identify up to three others to support the facilitation of smaller group work, or to identify a lead for each of the company goals you will be discussing.

4 Send invitations to participants – an example of the goals of the workshop is included below (see 'Hints and tips'). Be clear in your communications about the purpose of the workshop and what role you want participants to play through the workshop.

5 Go shopping – you need quite a few bits of 'kit' to run the workshop. A shopping list is provided as a guide in 'Hints and tips', below, but work through the agenda and think practically about what you need.

6 Similarly, be prepared with your poster prints and flipcharts. Getting groups to work together around a flipchart is great, but the impact is only useful for about four or five people maximum. Instead, get large A0-size posters printed that they can work around.

7 Prepare your CEO or most senior attending manager to provide an opening welcome speech – this will set the tone for the workshop, guide people on what is about to happen, and provide a relevant business context.

Running the workshop – introduction (15–30 minutes)

8   As participants arrive – give them a random card with a number (1–5) – this will indicate which number table they sit at. This allows you to mix up the groups randomly and start to encourage cross-team interaction.

9   Welcome participants and outline the purpose of the workshop and what the business hopes to get from it.

10 Mood board (see Section 2): ask participants to use the red dots to indicate where they feel their level of knowledge is for the three prepared statements – (I understand the company goals; I understand how my team can contribute best to the goals; I know what I need to do to deliver those goals).

11 You may want to run an ice-breaker to get people energized, or talking to others in the organization who they don't know so well.

12 CEO to formally introduce the workshop: set the scene to the group in plenary by describing the business challenge ahead, the need for everyone to work in an aligned way, and giving their best at all times – and the desire for everyone to get involved in determining and delivering organizational success.

13 Facilitator introduces the workshop: briefly explain the workshop activities, what they need from people and what the participants can expect.

14 Introduce the graffiti wall – at any time, a participant can write a comment, question, opinion, draw a picture, etc on the graffiti wall – it will be reviewed at the end by the leadership team (see 'Graffiti wall' in Section 3).

Running the workshop – familiarization with company goals (15 minutes)

15 In the table groups, review the preprinted cards that show the company goals. Encourage groups to discuss and agree what this might mean, why it is important, who it impacts, etc. This activity is intended to simply familiarize the groups with the company goals in preparation for the workshop. If you identified a lead person for each goal, encourage them to rotate around the groups to answer questions and offer clarifications.

Running the workshop – contribution to goals (15 minutes)

16 Split into functional teams in break-out areas. Provide each team with a preprinted A0 poster that shows four quadrants (see Figure 14.1, below, 'Poster – agreeing contribution'). With each of the overall company goals printed on separate cards, ask the teams to review the company goal cards, and stick them in the appropriate quadrant to identify how that team will contribute to each goal.

17 Once each team has completed the poster, the team leader or functional manager presents how s/he sees the alignment – and takes challenges from the group.

Running the workshop – team initiatives (30 minutes)

18 Staying in the functional teams, provide each team with a preprinted A0 poster that shows the company goals (see Figure 14.2, below, 'Poster – team initiatives'). The company goals are ideally preprinted onto this chart so that everyone has the same ones.

19 The team should highlight and discuss any projects or initiatives that support the company goals. These might be things that are under way, or might be new ideas or suggestions about activities they could start to contribute to company goals. These should all be noted on the poster.

20 The functional manager or team leader should challenge and question the group so that they feel they have a robust set of initiatives. The team should consider questions such as:
   – Are we doing enough/trying to do too much?
   – Do we have full alignment – are there things we are doing that do not connect to the goals?
   – Are there any significant gaps between us and the goals?
   – Are there any low-value activities that will not have much impact? Should we postpone anything?
   – Are the priorities right? Are there quick wins? Can we identify high-value initiatives?
   – Are we realistic? Can we deliver this?

21 The team should capture their general comments or reflections at the bottom section of the poster.

Running the workshop – the gallery review (30 minutes)

22 Provide each functional team with a preprinted A0 poster that shows a quadrant with opportunity to comment (see Figure 14.3, below, 'Poster – gallery review'). Ask the functional teams to stick up the poster next to their 'Contribution' and 'Team initiatives' posters and provide one representative from the team to stay with their own posters.

23 Ask the different functional teams to 'walkabout' and look at the initiatives defined for each of the other functions. Encourage them to post questions/challenges/comments to the other functions by writing comments on the poster – whether it be the comments; opportunities to collaborate (ie where functions, sub-teams or individuals could offer support or work together, or where they have a similar challenge); potential conflicts (ie where one initiative or idea seems to pull against the requirements of another – maybe in terms of goal, resources required, etc); and, finally, any other dependencies (ie does one initiative require the completion or outcome of another?). This part of the process enables teams to identify where they might work together for a better outcome, or where there is risk of conflict or duplication. Allow time for this process, and make sure that all participants do get around all of the other teams' charts.

24 When finished, the functional teams return to review the comments/challenges made by others – and will take those away for post-workshop discussion.

Running the workshop – functional review (15 minutes)

25 The functional teams should regroup and review the comments/challenges made by others. The focus should be on looking at opportunities to collaborate and mitigate against conflicting goals. No direct action need be taken at this time, but the points raised should be taken into account post-workshop.

Running the workshop – individual reflections/commitment card (15 minutes)

26 Allow time for individuals to reflect personally. Take time to allow them to consider the outputs to date, and write on the commitment card (see Section 1) what they personally can contribute to the business, or how they plan to support the objectives – either with WHAT they will do, or HOW they will operate.

Running the workshop – pulling it all together (30 minutes)

27 The lead for each goal should have identified and noted which functions directly and indirectly contribute to this target, and gathered some themes from the different teams about their contributions to the overall goals. This is the opportunity for them to summarize what they are seeing related to their goal, fill in any gaps, and address any issues or questions. Each goal should be reviewed in just a few minutes – keep this section moving and interactive if you can. If you have not identified a lead for each goal, this can be done by the senior manager present (eg CEO).

28 Each participant is then asked to put their name on a post-it note and add it to one of the initiatives that they would like to contribute to or get involved in outside of their normal functional area. These should be followed up after the workshop – they help to break down silos and promote cross-team collaboration.

Reviewing the workshop – mood board and graffiti wall (10 minutes)

29 Ask participants to use the green dots to indicate where they feel their level of knowledge is FOLLOWING THE WORKSHOP for the three prepared statements – (I understand the company goals; I understand how my team can contribute best to the goals; I know what I need to do to deliver those goals). Invite participants to provide feedback on the workshop using the graffiti wall.

Workshop close (10 minutes)

30 Thank participants for their attendance and for their participative and constructive involvement and explain the next steps that will be taken or that the teams need to take for themselves. This might include functional or team reviews of workshop outputs, and one-to-one objective setting sessions, to put a structure and a focus on aligned performance for the coming year.

Post-workshop

31 Consolidate the workshop outcomes. It is usually more practical to ask team leads or functional managers to summarize their own outcomes, but you will also need to summarize the collective outputs and tell the story of the workshop in follow-up communications. Ensure that managers and employees alike follow up on opportunities to collaborate and on setting individual objectives.

32 Keeping the workshop outcomes alive and relevant after the event is important in order to retain its credibility. Talk about it in your team briefings and other regular communications, and ensure that you track progress.

33 You may want to cascade the outcomes to the next level of employee throughout your whole organization, following the same process but with the outputs from the leadership workshop becoming the inputs for the all-employee workshop.

34 Consider holding a stand-up (see Section 2) the following day, just to reflect on the workshop, take feedback, ideas and suggestions and consider how to maintain the energy from that day.

Summary timetable for the workshop:

- Introduction (15–30 minutes)
- Familiarization with company goals (15 minutes)
- Contribution to goals (15 minutes)
- Team initiatives (30 minutes)
- The gallery review (30 minutes)
- Functional review (15 minutes)
- Individual reflections (15 minutes)
- Pulling it all together (30 minutes)
- Mood board and graffiti wall (10 minutes)
- Workshop close (10 minutes)

Hints and tips

- Good briefings to your senior managers or functional leads will be important to get the best out of the workshop.
- You might want to consider booking a professional photographer for the workshop. A set of reportage photographs from the event can be useful to remind people about it, to capture teamwork and engagement in action and to use in future communications.
- Some draft goals to use in your communications about the session are included below.

At the end of the workshop, you will have:

- Discussed the company goals and values – and maybe improved your understanding of these.
- Reviewed your team's commitment to the goals, and developed some team objectives aligned to them.
- Viewed the commitments of other teams to the goals, and identified opportunities for collaboration and/or conflict avoidance.
- Made personal commitments to the delivery of success for the company.

An equipment shopping list (for a workshop of 30 people):

- 30 cards numbered 1–5 on different coloured card;
- a graffiti wall preprinted;

- three mood boards preprinted;
- coloured dots 100 × red and 100 × green;
- five sets of cards, with each card in each set describing one of the company's key goals;
- a set of cards showing key goals or initiatives for each function;
- five rolls of paper;
- 30 × large Post-it notepads;
- 30 × marker pens;
- self-adhesive spray;
- Blu-tack;
- masking tape;
- five dialogue sheets preprinted;
- five RACI quadrant sheets preprinted;
- comments/challenges charts for the gallery view;
- 30 × individual commitment cards – preprinted.

Some poster templates

Figure 14.1 Poster – agreeing contribution

Overall Responsibility Do we set the targets, measure and report?	Directly contributing Do we have a role that will have a clear impact on the target?
Indirectly contributing Do we have a role that supports the delivery of the target?	Maintaining Awareness If we can't contribute, will we maintain awareness of the target and achievement?

Figure 14.2   Poster – team initiatives

Company Goal	Functional/Team Initiatives
Functional Reflections	

Figure 14.3   Poster – gallery review

Initial Thoughts and Reactions	Opportunities to Collaborate/Support
Potential Conflicts	Dependencies with Other Projects/Initiatives

Evaluation

The mood boards and the graffiti wall are effective ways to capture in-the-moment feedback about how people felt about the workshop process, their level of engagement and the value they have taken from it.

You can also consider some less direct indicators of success, such as the degree of interaction, how much discussion and challenge there was, and whether the department heads took away some useful feedback on the direction, goals and objectives.

You might also consider some of the core objectives of the workshop and, over time, review how these have been met, by considering how many opportunities for collaboration were identified and subsequently acted upon, or how many issues or boundary infringements were discussed and avoided. You may also get a sense of the degree to which silos have begun to break down.

Ultimately, the aim of the workshops is to get everyone behind delivery of the company's goals, so consideration of the line of sight of objectives, the degree of achievement and the company's success have to be taken into account when determining whether 'making connections' was a valuable process.

Evaluating your engagement initiatives 15

Why measure success?

Throughout this book the importance of evaluation has been highlighted. In the Introduction, it was mentioned that there may be little point in utilizing any of these tools if you have little interest or time for evaluation of their effectiveness, and that there is always a risk of misjudging your audience and switching them off, rather than on, with your use of interventions. Without evaluation, how would you ever know? And so to that end, each tool is provided with some guidance or prompt questions about what and how to evaluate its impact. In some cases this is at different levels of evaluation from a high level of face validity (did participants enjoy it?) to a fuller organizational effectiveness review (did it impact on your bottom line?). The evaluation of each individual tool, and of some of them used synergistically, will provide you with a 'point in time' assessment of the engagement spike created (or otherwise!) by a particular initiative.

However, you should be concerned about the overall levels of engagement among your employees. The tools in this book strive to deliver not a one-off spike, but by their continued use, variety and stretch across organization levels and functional specialities, they aim to bring about an ongoing level of commitment among your workforce. Earlier commentary in the introductory sections highlighted the importance of engagement because of its impact on motivation, productivity and ultimately profitability. With such benefits as this as an outcome, you will no doubt want to make it a priority to understand the overall, and the ongoing, levels of engagement in your business.

Employee opinion surveys and benchmarking

If your business has the funding, and the time, there is no better way to assess your engagement, and to benchmark it, than seeking out the services of a professional services organization that specialises in just that. The advantages are clear – highly qualified organizational specialist expertise, years of experience of working with companies large and small, rigorous statistical analysis and solid benchmarks with companies just like yours, and very different to yours. In most cases you will also find that survey providers are willing and able (some even encourage) to adapt surveys to meet your business requirements – although this is limited by a requirement to benchmark. The level of support you can expect can range from delivery of a survey or evaluation, right through to analysis and communication of results and implementation of improvement plans and they can offer expertise, insight and ideas at every stage of that journey. It is a commitment though – to be able to demonstrate progress or value for money you probably need to invest in a continual review process at least every two years.

The costs, however, are likely to be high. It is difficult to quantify, as different suppliers will take different approaches, and there are key dependencies that will include your organization size, geography, responses rates, etc. It is likely that for a robust survey that meets your specific needs, you will need to invest in excess of £10,000 and, as such, it could be considered that the professional survey really targets the larger organizations. That said, it is possible to create a solid business case for the investment, if you can demonstrate that increased levels of engagement will lead to some of the benefits described earlier (increased productivity, for example).

Local 'temperature' checks

Using smaller-scale surveys and questionnaires that you can facilitate and collate internally will provide you with some information about your success in driving engagement. You can do this by using the mood board tool as one simple mechanism to obtain a quantitative response. Alternatively you could consider using a graffiti wall, asking a specific question about engagement for qualitative responses. For a longer survey or a more detailed set of information, try a simple online survey creation tool such as SurveyMonkey, or even a simple printed questionnaire.

One of the quickest methods to get a response or to take a temperature check is the use of 'voting buttons'. This uses voting buttons on e-mails to request responses (usually an option within your normal e-mail program). The disadvantage of this approach is that it takes time to collate responses, as they come to the recipient as separate e-mail responses from each individual. In a large organization this could be logistically challenging, but in smaller organizations, or for smaller sample groups, it can be effective. The simplicity of the approach and the ease with which an immediate response can be sent may prompt a good return rate.

Focus groups

On a much smaller scale, you can run focus groups to assess the overall level of engagement in your organization. This is a great opportunity to hear feedback directly from employees about how your initiatives are improving engagement and what more could be done.

You need a capable facilitator and an open mind. You need a briefing and scope for the discussion that focuses on positives and opportunities and does not turn into a negative or complaints-focused session. You also need to ensure that your focus group is engaged in action and joint accountability rather than blame or on pushing actions and decisions upwards. Keep in mind what you, the facilitator and the participants can realistically influence, and focus on those issues and suggestions.

External validation

If the professionally serviced employee opinion survey is out of your price range, it is not a dead end. If you want to see how you measure there are some other external validation surveys that you may want to consider participating in, which might include:

- Great Place to Work;
- Sunday Times Best Companies;
- Investors in People.

Great Place to Work (GPTW) and Sunday Times Best Companies (STBC) lists both feature segmentation for company size, and some other segmentation such as geography (GPTW) or not for profit (STBC), whilst the Investors in People standard is highly adaptable to all sizes and types of organization.

Whilst there are typically fees involved in the assessment and development processes associated with each, it is an opportunity to have your organization 'audited' and provides you with some benchmark, showing how you measure up to others. Your management practices, the views of your employees and the details of your practices and policies will be examined and reviewed, Do not expect to 'win' or to be featured as one of the top categories, but enter into it with a view to understanding how you are perceived and how you compare.

Celebrate success

Most of all, celebrate your successes. When engagement is good, and business is good, there is no better time to throw a party!

Quick view of tools and templates

16

Quick view – top tools

Table 16.1 is designed to help you to select, at a glance, the right tools for your engagement needs.

Table 16.1 Quick view of tools

	Quick	Cheap	In situ	Big groups	Small teams	Individual
	Less than 1 hour	Minimal cost	At workspace	12+	Max 12	
Analogies	•	•		•	•	
Artistry	•	•			•	
Back to the floor		•	•			
Benchmarking roadtrip		•			•	
Birthday breakfast	•	•			•	
Celebrating career		•	•			•
Change champions		•	•		•	•
Chew and chat	•	•	•		•	
Clear objectives		•	•			
Columnist			•	•	•	
Commitment cards	•	•	•	•	•	
Common cause		•		•	•	

(Continued)

Table 16.1 (*Continued*)

	Quick	Cheap	In situ	Big groups	Small teams	Individual
	Less than 1 hour	*Minimal cost*	*At workspace*	*12+*	*Max 12*	
Communicate, communicate, communicate		•		•	•	
Communities of practice		•			•	
Compelling brand				•		
Connecting lessons		•			•	
Customer experience		•			•	•
Dialogue sheets	•	•			•	
Dream clouds	•	•			•	
Enablement			•			•
Farewell letter	•	•	•			•
Find a friend	•	•	•	•	•	•
Following the flow		•			•	•
Graffiti wall	•	•	•	•	•	
Hello hamper		•	•			•
High performing teams	•	•			•	
Hot topics	•	•			•	
Idea hub			•		•	
Idea wall	•	•	•		•	
Inclusive selection		•			•	
Inspiring cinema club			•	•	•	
Keep in touch	•	•	•			•
Letter from the top	•	•	•			•
Light bites	•	•	•		•	
Making connections				•		•

(*Continued*)

Table 16.1 *(Continued)*

	Quick	Cheap	In situ	Big groups	Small teams	Individual
	Less than 1 hour	*Minimal cost*	*At workspace*	*12+*	*Max 12*	
Marketplace				•		
Media training					•	
Mentoring		•	•			•
Mood boards	•	•	•	•	•	
Peer post	•	•	•	•	•	•
Pinspiration board	•	•	•	•	•	
Preparing for change (P4C)		•		•	•	
Progress bar	•	•	•	•	•	
Re-enable		•	•			•
Re-engage		•	•			•
Roadshow				•	•	
Shadowing the customer		•			•	•
Stand-up	•	•	•		•	
Top team representative		•				
Top team unplugged		•	•	•	•	

Some additional templates

Table 16.2 provides an example of a typical 'happy sheet' evaluation form.

Table 16.2   A typical 'happy sheet'

Title of the workshop or course	Name of the workshop facilitator/ trainer
Date	Location

Please indicate your level of agree with the statements listed below:

	Strongly Agree	Agree	Neutral	Disagree
The course/workshop was relevant to my needs/my job				
The objectives of the course/ workshop were met				
The course/workshop followed a logical structure				
Materials used and provided were of good quality and relevant to the content				
There was sufficient time for this workshop/training				
I enjoyed the course/workshop				
The trainer/facilitator was knowledgeable				
The trainer/facilitator was well prepared				
The location and room were adequate for this workshop/training				
The facilities and refreshments were good				
What did you like most about today's event?				
What could make it even better?				
What are your main takeaways from today's event?				
Any other comments				

Facilitation planning

The template in Table 16.3 is designed to help you to plan an intervention that you have been asked to facilitate. The questions are designed for you to ask the client to get clarity on the scope and objectives of the session, and to help you plan the intervention to deliver against those. The questions are not exhaustive, you may have other questions that you need to ask – or there may be some questions on the checklist that are not relevant – but it should act as a guide to get you started.

Table 16.3 Facilitation planning template

Context
Who is the 'client'? Who wants this event to happen?
How has the need for this session come about?
Why have you determined the need for external facilitation?
Is there any business context that is particularly relevant to the session? Are there any big changes happening?
Are there any 'no-go' topics/areas? Anything to be sensitive about?
Is there senior sponsorship from this session? Who – and where – in the organization? Why are they interested?
What role do you expect the 'leader' to play? Is he or she part of the team, or is he or she stepping back or out?

Objectives/purpose
What are you hoping to get out of the session? Describe both the explicit outcomes and any underlying or added-value outcomes.
What does success look like?
Can you specify the specific objectives and outcomes of the session?

(Continued)

Table 16.3   *(Continued)*

Objectives/purpose
How would you prioritize them?
Are you anticipating delivery of any 'products' from this session?

Style/approach
Is the preference for a formal approach, or informal?
What style has worked well with this team/this function in the past?
Are there any tools/techniques that are particularly favoured?
Are there any tools or approaches that have been used before that did not really have an impact with the team?
How should the session approach be signed off – checked when and by who?
Who will take responsibility for taking notes/writing up outcomes, etc?
Would they expect – or be OK with – pre-work?

Attendees
Who will attend the meeting?
Are they eager to attend? What concerns are there?
How has this session been presented to them?
What are their collective expectations?
Can I contact them individually in advance of the session to discuss their individual expectations?

Logistics
Confirm the dates of the session.
Will this be a one-off, or a series of workshops?

Table 16.3 *(Continued)*

Logistics
Is the meeting venue, etc, arranged? Check that it has all the facilities that are required (eg break-out rooms, flipcharts, multimedia, etc).
What do I need to bring with me?
What breaks will be required?

Other notes

REFERENCES

Best Companies (2015) [accessed 24 February 2017] [Online] http://blog.b.co.uk/blog/the-spirit-of-innovation-create-an-entrepreneurial-buzz-in-your-workplace

Bridger, E (2014) *Employee Engagement*, vol. 10, Kogan Page, London

CIPD Factsheet (2015) [accessed 24 February 2017] Employee Engagement [Online] https://www.cipd.co.uk/knowledge/fundamentals/relations/engagement/factsheet

CIPD Factsheet (2016a) [accessed 24 February 2017] Change Management [Online] www.cipd.co.uk/hr-resources/factsheets/change-management.aspx

CIPD Factsheet (2016b) [accessed 24 February 2017] Employee Communication [Online] www.cipd.co.uk/knowledge/fundamentals/relations/communication/factsheet

CIPD Factsheet (2016c) [accessed 24 February 2017] Employer Brand [Online] www.cipd.co.uk/knowledge/fundamentals/people/recruitment/brand-factsheet#7132

Cirillo, F (2006) The pomodoro technique (the pomodoro), *Agile Processes in Software Engineering*, **54** (2)

Clutterbuck, D and Megginson, D (1999) *Mentoring Executives and Directors*, Routledge, London

Fulham, R (2016) [accessed 24 February 2017] 30% of New Starters Plan to Leave Within a Year, *HR Grapevine* [Online] www.hrgrapevine.com/content/article/2016-07-05-30-of-new-starters-plan-to-leave-within-a-year

Gallup (2011–12) [accessed 24 February 2017] Worldwide, 13% of Employees are Engaged at Work [Online] http://www.gallup.com/poll/165269/worldwide-employees-engaged-work.aspx

Germain, D and Reed, R (2009) *A Book About Innocent*, Penguin, London

Houle, S and Campbell, K (2016) [accessed 24 February 2017] What High-Quality Job Candidates Look for in a Company, *Gallup Business Journal* [Online] www.gallup.com/businessjournal/187964/high-quality-job-candidates-look-company.aspx

Leary-Joyce, J (2004) *Becoming an Employer of Choice: Making your organization a place where people want to work*, Chartered Institute of Personnel and Development, London

MacLeod, D and Clarke, N (2009) *Engaging for Success: Enhancing performance through employee engagement – a report to government*, Department for Business, Innovation and Skills, London

Network for Good [accessed 24 February 2017] [Online] www.networkforgood.com/corporate-tools/

Novak, D (2016) [accessed 24 February 2017] Recognizing Employees is the Simplest Way to Improve Morale, *Harvard Business Review* [Online] https://hbr.org/2016/05/recognizing-employees-is-the-simplest-way-to-improve-morale

Personnel Today (2011) [accessed 24 February 2017] Weekly Dilemma: Elections for Employee Representatives [Online] www.personneltoday.com/hr/weekly-dilemma-elections-for-employee-representatives/

Pollard, C (2015) [accessed 24 February 2017] 5 Reasons Why You Need to Get Media Training, *Huffington Post* [Online] www.huffingtonpost.com/catriona-pollard/5-reasons-why-you-need-to_2_b_7148624.html

Robinson, D, Perryman, S and Hayday, S (2004) *The Drivers of Employee Engagement*, Report-Institute for Employment Studies

Watson, L (2015) [accessed 24 February 2017] Humans Have Shorter Attention Span than Goldfish, Thanks to Smartphones, *Daily Telegraph* [Online] www.telegraph.co.uk/science/2016/03/12/humans-have-shorter-attention-span-than-goldfish-thanks-to-smart/

Werhane, W and Royal, M (2009) *Engaging and Enabling Employees for Company Success*, Hay Group's Employee Research, Workspan, pp 39–43

Woollaston, V (2015) [accessed 24 February 2017] How Often Do YOU Check Your Phone?, *MailOnline* [Online] www.dailymail.co.uk/sciencetech/article-3294994/How-check-phone-Average-user-picks-device-85-times-DAY-twice-realise.html

INDEX

Italics indicate a figure or table.